Electric Toy Making for Amateurs

This work treats of the making of electrical toys, electrical apparatus, motors, dynamos, and instruments in general, and is designed to bring within the reach of young and old the manufacture of genuine and useful electrical appliances.

BY

T. O'CONOR SLOANE, A.M., E.M., Ph.D.

AUTHOR OF

Standard Electrical Dictionary, Electricity Simplified,
Arithmetic of Electricity, etc., etc.

**Fredonia Books
Amsterdam, The Netherlands**

Electric Toy Making for Amateurs

by
T. O'Conor Sloane

ISBN: 1-4101-0793-0

Copyright © 2005 by Fredonia Books

Reprinted from the 1909 edition

Fredonia Books
Amsterdam, The Netherlands
http://www.fredoniabooks.com

All rights reserved, including the right to reproduce this book, or portions thereof, in any form.

In order to make original editions of historical works available to scholars at an economical price, this facsimile of the original edition of 1909 is reproduced from the best available copy and has been digitally enhanced to improve legibility, but the text remains unaltered to retain historical authenticity.

PREFACE.

ELECTRIC TOY MAKING is a very comprehensive title, one which may be made to embrace far more ground than this work pretends to cover. In the realms of amateur work of all kinds—mechanics, natural science, and even legerdemain or natural magic—electricity can be made to play an important part. The methods of applying it to simple constructions, within the reach and scope of amateurs, constitute the theme of this book. The effort has been to present the reader with a suggestive line of experimentation and construction, and to open a field within which his own ideas can have indefinite scope and extent. It is believed that little in the way of actual toy making can be done outside of the general limits here defined. Thus, as adjuncts to a static electric machine, Holtz or Wimshurst, a quantity of pieces of apparatus might have been described, but such appliances do not deserve to be called toys in any sense.

It is hoped that the work will prove fertile in the suggestive sense. Many things are presented which are susceptible of almost any quantity of modifications. The motors have been selected with regard to their variation from the usual type of "reversible dynamo."

The simple experiments and constructions given under static electricity are made, as far as possible, independent in action, except as far as an induction or spark coil and battery may be needed to operate some of them.

As a good workman is known by his tools, so is the electrician judged by his battery. The few hints given as to the use of batteries should tend to put the amateur on a proper footing at the all-important foundation and basis of his operations. With a well-kept battery the neatly constructed apparatus will appear to double advantage, and its effectiveness will be secured. Apparatus is often blamed for the shortcomings of the current-generator.

PREFACE TO THE NINETEENTH EDITION.

The success of the previous editions of this book has led the author to revise, and at the same time add several new chapters to the work, bringing it up-to-date, and giving further directions for the making of many interesting electrical contrivances.

I desire to express my thanks for the many favorable notices received from the press, as well as for many letters from students of Electricity.

THE AUTHOR.

CONTENTS.

CHAPTER I.

BATTERIES.

Primary Batteries in General—Batteries with Electric Light Carbons—A Tomato Can Battery—Materials for Battery Cells 9

CHAPTER II.

PERMANENT MAGNETS.

How to Magnetize Steel Bars—Rolling Armatures—Mahomet's Coffin—Magnetic Jack-straws—The Magnetic Top—The Magnetic Pendulum—Mayer's Floating Needles—Magnetic Fishes, and the Magnetic Swan, Boat, etc.... 23

CHAPTER III.

ELECTRO-MAGNETS.

Construction of Electro-Magnets—Magnetizing Coils—The Magic Circle—Magnetic Hemispheres............... 37

CHAPTER IV.

ELECTRIC MOTORS.

Pendulum Coil Motor—Recordon Magnet Motor—Multipolar Motor—Page's Rotating Armature—The Electric Locomotive... 46

CONTENTS.

CHAPTER V.

ELECTRIC BELLS.

The Tolling Bell—The Vibrating Bell—The Safe Protector 65

CHAPTER VI.

MISCELLANEOUS TOYS.

The Electric Dancer—The Magic Drum—The Electric Hammer—Electric Insects—The Incandescent Lamp 73

CHAPTER VII.

SPARK AND INDUCTION COILS, AND ALLIED SUBJECTS.
The Spark Coil—The Induction Coil—Recordon's Induction Coil—The Magneto-Generator—Electric Artillery—Electric Gymnastics—Ano-Kato—Simple Experiments in Static Electricity 89

CHAPTER VIII.

HAND POWER DYNAMO.

Page 121

CHAPTER IX.

An Easily Constructed Motor—Simple Electric Motor—A Small Electro Motor—Another Simple Motor—Simple Electric Locomotive Motor—Telegraph Key—Sounder — Microphone — Telephone Receiver 128

CHAPTER X.

MISCELLANEOUS RECEIPTS AND FORMULÆ.

Page 166

CHAPTER I.

BATTERIES.

PRIMARY BATTERIES IN GENERAL—BATTERIES WITH ELECTRIC LIGHT CARBONS—A TOMATO CAN BATTERY—MATERIALS FOR BATTERY CELLS.

Primary Batteries in General.

THE requirements of a good battery are easier stated than secured. It should be constant, of low resistance, and of good electro-motive force. The latter factor should not fall below one volt. For this reason the caustic soda batteries are hardly to be recommended unless the amateur is willing to use a large number of cells.

For constancy and cheapness the sulphate of copper cells lead. The quality of cheapness appertains both to original cost and expense of running. A great objection is their high resistance; for this reason a very large battery may seem to have but little power. If an effort is made to reduce their resistance, by bringing the plates closer, copper is deposited on the zinc.

The deposition of copper on the positive plates is not only annoying, as exacting scraping and cleaning, but exhausts the solutions. It does not do to bring the plates too close together.

This is one reason for high resistance, but there is a greater one. It is that the solutions either of zinc or copper sulphate in the cell are never of low resistance. Such solutions do not compare with dilute sulphuric acid for conductivity.

Owing to its constancy and cheapness, the sulphate of copper combinations form favorite batteries with telegraph operators. In the Daniell battery a plate of zinc is contained in a porous cup surrounded by a plate of copper The three are placed in a glass jar A solution of zinc sulphate is poured into the porous cup; a solution of copper sulphate into the outer jar. In the gravity battery only the glass jar and two plates are used. The copper plate is in the bottom and a gutta-percha covered wire leads from it. The zinc plates are near the top of the jar. To charge it, water is introduced until the zinc is covered. A handful of crystals of copper sulphate are added with a little zinc sulphate solution if necessary. Gravity is here relied on to keep the two solutions separate; the zinc sulphate increases in quantity with the working of the battery, but the copper sulphate solution is kept as strong as possible. After a while the zinc sulphate solution will exceed in specific gravity the copper sulphate solution, when the battery will cease to act properly. Hence, the upper layers of liquid are withdrawn from time to time and replaced by plain water.

The Leclanché battery, before the introduction of

BICHROMATE BATTERIES.

the dry batteries, was the great open circuit battery.

For intermittent work either type can now be recommended. For constant and heavy work neither is of any utility whatever.

For heavy work the bichromate cells are the best, all things considered. They are not very constant and with a heavy output soon begin to run down.

Of them the Bunsen battery is to be recommended for constant currents of long duration. The cell consists, in brief, of a porous cup and outer jar. In on of the divisions an amalgamated zinc plate is contained; in the other division a carbon plate. The carbon is surrounded by a strong solution of chromic and sulphuric acids. The latter imparts conductivity; the former is the depolarizer. The zinc is surrounded with dilute sulphuric acid. The two solutions inevitably diffuse one into the other. The more they are kept distinct the better the condition of the battery is.

The plain bichromate battery consists of a jar containing the amalgamated zinc and carbon plates and charged with the chromic-sulphuric acid solution. This is a defective combination. The chromic acid acts upon the zinc, and the battery rapidly deteriorates when on open circuit.

The latter trouble is avoided by removing the plates, or, at any rate, the zinc plate, when the cell is not in use. This practise economizes solution and is by all means to be recommended. Various mechanical constructions have been adopted for raising the plates. Such batteries are termed dip batteries.

The solution to be used should be carefully prepared. An inferior mixture gives very inferior results. The following is the celebrated Trouvé solution and can be highly recommended:

It requires—

Water	8 pints.
Powdered Potassium Bichromate	1 2-10 lbs.
Concentrated Sulphuric Acid	3 6-10 lbs.

The bichromate is added to the water and stirred well through it. The acid is slowly added, with constant stirring. A glass rod, and glass, or well enamelled iron vessels should be used for the mixing. As the acid is added the temperature rises and all, or nearly all, of the bichromate dissolves. Sometimes to four parts of water as much as one part of bichromate is added, with nearly two parts of sulphuric acid. All parts are by weight. The secret is in the fine pulverization of the bichromate and in the gradual addition with constant stirring of the acid.

Great care should be taken in pulverizing the bichromate to inhale none of the dust, as it may cause ulcers.

The above solution may be employed in the carbon plate division of the Bunsen cell with excellent results.

SAL AMMONIAC BATTERIES.

For the zinc plate division of the Bunsen cell, one part, by weight, of sulphuric acid to twelve of water is used.

Very useful little batteries may be constructed by using a mixture of two parts sal ammoniac with one part of mercurous or white mercury sulphate in water as the excitant. Zinc and carbon are the elements and are contained in a single cell.

A piece of old battery carbon may be bored out for part of its length and used as both the cup and negative element at once. It should be well paraffined by dipping in melted paraffine wax. A zinc rod or wire small enough to enter the hole having some rubber bands wound around it, is inserted as the positive plate. The bands must cover as little of its surface as possible and its bottom must not touch the carbon. The sal ammoniac-mercurous sulphate solution is the excitant. A little of the mixture is placed in the cup, some water is added and mixed with it. The zinc is placed in position, and all is ready for use.

Such a battery is, of course, more of a curiosity than a practical source of current.

For working small apparatus the silver chloride cell has been very highly thought of. Although originally of somewhat high cost the silver is not lost and can readily be reconverted into chloride when the battery becomes exhausted.

A test tube made of extra thick glass will answer for the cell. A piece of sheet zinc is bent so as to fit closely in the tube, in contact with its sides. A lug or projecting piece extends up from the zinc. The plate should be nearly as long as the tube. It must be well amalgamated and put in position.

Next, a very thin piece of silver foil is wrapped around a rod of wood the size of a lead pencil. A silver wire is soldered or otherwise connected to this to act as terminal. A thick paste of silver chloride and water is spread upon a piece of blotting paper, which is just long enough to go once around the silver. This is then wrapped around the foil with the chloride paste against the silver.

A strip of muslin is wrapped two or three times around the blotting paper and is neatly sewed or tied.

A thick rubber band, best a section from some rather heavy gas tubing, is put over each end of the silver element. It must fit without squeezing. A perforated slice of cork will answer as well. The silver element is dropped into place, and the tube is filled with a solution of sal ammoniac in water.

Such a cell is without local action, and represents a very small open circuit battery. Two or three will operate a small induction coil. Their durability depends on the amount of silver chloride.

As no gas is generated, the cells may be enclosed hermetically by corks, coated or covered with a thick layer of sealing-wax or cap-cement. They form a convenient pocket battery. Sometimes they are made in soft rubber tubing, closed at both ends with corks and cement as above.

The present work does not purport to treat of batteries, yet it has seemed well to say this much on the subject and to give some examples of the utilization of common material for the purpose in the next sections.

For temporary purposes a battery of great power is easily made up by using the bichromate solution, with zinc and carbon as the elements, and any convenient porcelain or glass vessels as the cups or jars. For permanent batteries considerable may be done in the way of neat mounting, etc., to make them attractive objects to the eye of the amateur electrician.

One concluding word must be said : Never attempt to use unamalgamated zincs in a bichromate cell. To amalgamate, place a little globule of mercury in a saucer with some dilute sulphuric acid. Wet the zinc plate with the acid. Then, with a bit of zinc or galvanized iron, rub the mercury well over the surface of the zinc plate.

In the cut of the electric light carbon battery, page 18, the arrangements for amalgamating are shown. The slip of galvanized iron in the saucer is bent so as to fit around the circular zinc rods.

Batteries with Electric Light Carbons.

Electric light carbons make excellent material for the negative plate of batteries. They may be used in various ways as regards their mounting.

The first thing to be done to them is to remove the copper plating from such portions as are to be immersed in the acid or battery fluid. This is easily effected by immersion in dilute nitric acid to the desired depth. A few seconds will generally suffice to strip the metal.

The next step depends on how they are to be used. Old rejected pieces, such as the lamp trimmers throw away, may be employed in some constructions. If the pieces are short, an excellent system is the following:

For each battery jar one long piece is selected. The copper is removed from its lower part, one or two inches at one end being left plated. It is then washed and dried in an oven. To the upper or coppered end while still hot, or if it has cooled, while heated gently, paraffine wax is applied just below the copper, until the porous carbon has absorbed all that it can.

The smaller pieces of carbon are completely stripped of copper. The long piece is placed upright in a porous cup and the small pieces are packed in around it. This makes the negative element. The wire is wound around the coppered end and may, if desired, be soldered thereto. It is also possible to drill a small hole in the top and screw in a binding post, which may be further secured by soldering.

The illustration presents another method. To carry it out the carbons must be rather long, according to the average of the rejected pieces. The copper is dis-

NEGATIVE PLATES.

solved from their lower portions, leaving one or two inches coppered. They are washed, dried and paraffined as just described.

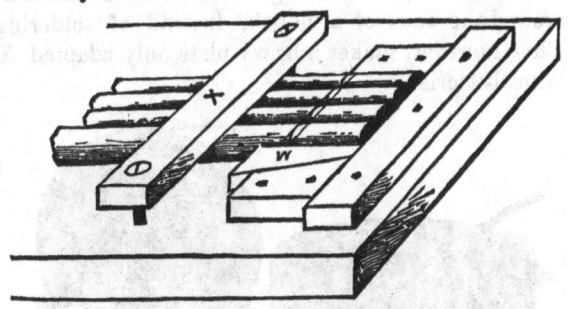

Fig. 1 — Making Negative Plates from Arc Light Carbons.

They are next placed on a board and secured as shown by a strip, X. As carbons are often slightly bent, care should be taken to turn them until they lie as fully in contact as possible. A couple of side blocks, abutting against a straight end piece, form a pocket to receive the coppered ends, which are pressed together by the wedge, W.

With soldering acid, solder and soldering iron, the ends are now soldered together. The solder is melted into the grooves formed by the contiguous carbons. After cooling, the carbons, now united, are turned over, are again secured as shown and the opposite sides are soldered.

This gives what is practically a solid battery plate, and which really possesses special advantages in its

18 *ELECTRIC TOY MAKING.*

increased area of surface. A binding post can be soldered into one of the grooves.

Another way of uniting carbons is to cast lead around the ends of a bunch, instead of soldering. This, however, makes a heavy plate only adapted for large batteries.

FIG. 2.—ELECTRIC LIGHT CARBON BATTERY.

An excellent method is illustrated in the next cut. It is to cut out a circular or square piece of wood to cover or else to simply extend across the top of the jar. Holes are bored in it through which the carbons are tightly thrust after stripping and paraffining. The ends are brought just flush with the surface of the wood, and a strip of brass or copper is sweated to the plated carbon ends. This is done by first tinning the lower surface of the brass plates, where it is to come in contact with the carbons, and then tinning each carbon top. The strip is now laid in position, and by heating it the two sets of tinned surfaces are caused to unite by the solder running together. The brass plate is pressed down and held so until the solder is partly cooled and has set or hardened.

If the ends are not plated a piece of copper foil can be forced into the hole with the carbon, and to this a wire is soldered connecting all the carbons together. The foil can be doubled over the top of the carbons, and the connecting strip of foil used as just described.

As regards zincs, old Leclanché battery zincs can be used in a similar way by thrusting them through holes in a board. All the soldering must be done before the zincs are amalgamated.

A very neat battery is made by cutting out the wood to cover the jar, and giving it a rebate all around its edge, so that it cannot slip. The zincs and carbons are then fastened in holes as just described. For a single fluid battery this is an excellent form of construction.

The wooden top may be made of pine, or, if a

hard wood is desired, mahogany or maple is good. Ash is not altogether satisfactory, because if the lower surface gets wet the piece warps badly. But this is of less importance, as the greatest care should be taken to avoid such wetting as the acid will corrode the connections.

It will be seen also that a binding post can in this battery be screwed through a hole in the brass or copper strips directly into the wood, and then, if desired, may be soldered.

A Tomato Can Battery.

The above designation applies to a simple form of home-made battery in which a discarded tomato can may be made to play a part. It is a battery of considerable merit, but of too low voltage.

The outer vessel for containing the fluids and other parts of the battery is a tomato can or other iron vessel. Within it is a porous cup. The annular space between is filled with fine scrap iron, such as turnings, borings and clippings. A zinc plate goes into the porous cup.

The exciting solution is a ten per cent. solution of caustic soda. The wires are connected as shown, one to the zinc plate and one to the can itself.

The battery is liable to polarization, but the large surface of the iron protects it to some extent.

If it is desired to make it constant or self-depolarizing, a quantity of oxide of copper may be placed in the bottom of the jar upon a layer of iron borings and the rest of the filling of iron scraps may be dispensed

FIG 3. A TOMATO CAN BATTERY.

with. This makes it a Lalande-Chaperon battery. The E. M. F. is about .75 volt.

Materials for Battery Cells.

Before leaving the subject a word may be said on the cell proper. Porcelain marmalade jars make excellent receptacles for small couples. In selecting a vessel there is one point of special importance. The sides should not taper or slope outwards. It is far better to have a vessel that is smaller at the neck than at the bottom. Self-sealing preserve jars for this reason are very serviceable.

Wooden battery troughs have been used to a considerable extent. These may be made of pine, oak, mahogany or maple. The sides may be protected from the liquids by baking and, while hot, coating with melted paraffine. Potassium bichromate battery solution, however, will in time attack almost anything except glass or porcelain.

A long trough to contain a number of elements may have its partitions made of glass set in grooves in the sides and secured with cement.

CHAPTER II.
Permanent Magnets.

HOW TO MAGNETIZE STEEL BARS—ROLLING ARMATURES—MAHOMET'S COFFIN—MAGNETIC JACKSTRAWS—THE MAGNETIC TOP—THE MAGNETIC PENDULUM—MAYER'S FLOATING NEEDLES—MAGNETIC FISHES, AND THE MAGNETIC SWAN, BOAT, ETC.

How to Magnetize Steel Bars.

A BAR of soft iron held in a magnetic field, is acted on by the lines of force constituting the field, and becomes a magnet and will attract iron, and act exactly as the permanent magnet does. When removed from the field of force it will show hardly any magnetism. If a piece of steel is treated in the same way, it will also show magnetism when in the field; but, on removal, will retain some of it. It is a permanent magnet.

Permanent magnets are easily made of such material. The bar of steel should be of good quality, and tempered to a straw color or purple. All the shaping, filing or polishing, which it is proposed to give it, should be done before magnetizing, as the least thing in the way of filing or jarring the magnet injures its power.

24   ELECTRIC TOY MAKING.

It may be magnetized by another magnet, permanent or electro—or by a magnetizing coil and battery. It is enough to touch one end to the most strongly magnetic part of the field magnet of an active dynamo. This suffices because of the intense polarity of the powerfully excited machine.

With a single permanent magnet, a bar may be thus magnetized. It is rubbed from the centre to one end, with one pole of the magnet a number of times, the magnet being drawn away from the end and carried back to its centre through the air, and the stroking is repeated a number of times. Then the same process with the other pole of the magnet is applied to the other half of the bar. It is well to turn it over so as to stroke all sides of it.

A simpler way is to stroke from one end of the bar to the other, always in the same direction, with one pole of a magnet, returning it through the air.

Two magnets may be fixed in an inclined position with their poles of opposite name close together, and the bar may be stroked with them as described above for a single magnet. The next cut illustrates this method as well as the process next to be described.

FIG. 4. MAGNETIZING A BAR OF STEEL.

An excellent method is to apply the stroking from

MAGNETIZING HORSESHOE BARS.

centre to ends with two magnets simultaneously. A little bit of wood or brass should be used to prevent their ends from coming in contact in the centre of the magnet. The cut shows the arrangement, l representing the separating piece, and also shows the bar resting upon the opposite poles of two other magnets. The end to be stroked with a north pole should rest upon the north pole of a magnet, and the same applies to the south pole.

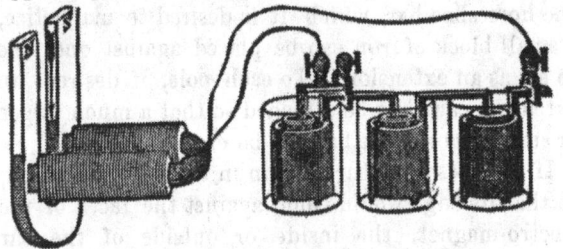

FIG. 5. MAGNETIZING A HORSESHOE MAGNET.

Magnets are generally either straight or horseshoe in shape. If of the latter description they may be magnetized by touching both poles to opposite poles of a dynamo field magnet. It should be noted that this will reduce for the moment the power of the dynamo. Where a small electro magnet is at hand the stroking process may be applied as shown in the cut. The bent bar is placed against the poles of the excited electro-magnet, and is drawn downwards as shown by the arrow. This is repeated a number of times and the bent bar, after each stroke, is pulled away from the electro-magnet and is returned to its original position. It is then well to reverse operations; to apply the other face of the bent bar, now partly magnetized, to the electro-magnet, but this time to keep the bend upwards as the opposed poles must be kept in the same relation. The bar is now drawn upwards and away from the electro-magnet a few times and the operation is complete.

If the electro-magnet has its poles too far apart to fit the horseshoe bar, which it is desired to magnetize, a small block of iron can be placed against one pole to set as an extension. To each pole, if desired, an extension can thus be attached so that a much larger or smaller horseshoe bar can be magnetized.

If the horseshoe bar is thin in the other direction, so that its edge would come against the faces of the electro-magnet, the inside or outside of the bar should be rubbed, and not the edges.

To make powerful magnets thin pieces of steel may be magnetized separately and then clamped or screwed together. They must not be rivetted or soldered as either would injure the magnetism.

Another way, Jacobi's method, to magnetize a horseshoe bar, is to place it with its poles against those of a strong horseshoe magnet. A bar of soft iron, long enough to reach across from outside to outside of the parallel legs is now laid across at or near the ends of the legs of the bar to be magnetized and is drawn along it back to the bend and away from it. It

MAGNETIZING WITH COILS.

is returned through the air and the process repeated a few times on each side of the bar. It is said that a one-pound magnet may thus be made which will carry twenty-six and a half pounds.

To magnetize with a coil, all that is necessary is to surround a part or all of the bar with a coil of insulated wire and to pass a strong current through it for an instant. By Elias' method the coil is moved backward and forward along the bar which it encircles while the current is passing. The number of passes is of greater importance for weak currents. For strong ones a single pass is ample.

By another method the bar is armed with two short cylinders of iron, one at each end of three or four times its diameter. These armatures should be of soft iron. It is placed in the axis of a coil that is of the same diameter as the armatures and which is long enough to include both armatures and the bar. A current is passed through the coil and powerful magnetization results.

To preserve magnets their opposite poles must be connected so as to complete the magnetic circuit. With bar magnets this is best done by placing them, almost touching each other, in pairs with their opposite poles corresponding in direction. Two little bars of soft iron laid across from pole to pole complete the circuit. Such bars are termed keepers. If a single magnet is in question a bent piece of soft iron may be used to connect the two poles. A magnet

ELECTRIC TOY MAKING.

may even be left without any keeper, if placed in the magnetic meridian. For horseshoe magnets a single keeper, the armature, suffices to connect both poles.

In using magnets all jarring must be avoided. It does no harm to pull the armature off if done perfectly steadily and without jar. The re-attraction of the armature with a "click," is what deteriorates a permanent magnet most rapidly.

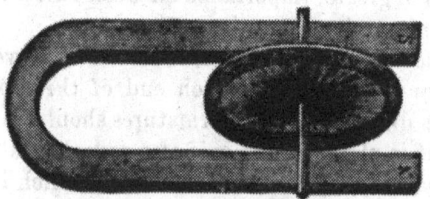

FIG. 6. THE ROLLING ARMATURE.

Rolling Armatures.

The rolling armature consists of a short cylindrical axis of iron to whose center a wheel is attached. The wheel may be made of lead or other metal. When it is placed as shown upon a horseshoe magnet it will adhere, but if the magnet is properly inclined will roll down to the end. The momentum of the fly-wheel keeps up the motion and the armature rolls across the poles and up the other side for a considerable distance.

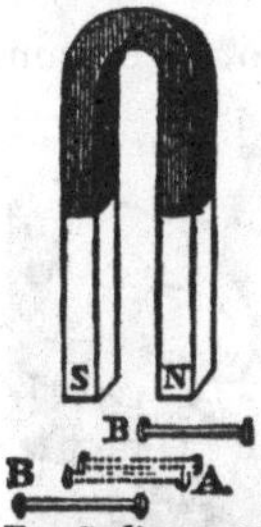

A modification of this armature consists of two little bars of iron with brass rollers attached to their ends. They are placed in the position A, as shown in the dotted lines in the cut. On approaching them with the magnet they become polarized both in the same sense and at once repel each other and roll away as shown by B B.

FIG. 7. REPULSION OF ROLLING ARMATURES.

If the horseshoe magnet has parallel sides, and the last described armatures are nicely made, they may be made to roll upon it somewhat as the other rolling armature does.

By concealing the magnet under a sheet of paper the recession or rolling away from each other of the two bars may be made to seem quite mysterious.

Mahomet's Coffin.

The next cut shows a very pretty magnetic experiment which recalls the famous unsupported coffin of Mahomet. A needle, whose point may be broken off, is magnetized by a few strokes with a magnet. On drawing it by a thread, as shown, over the poles of a horseshoe magnet so as to bring like poles over each other, it will lie horizontally and motionless in the air, sustained by an invisible force. As it is drawn forwards and from the further side of the horseshoe magnet it tends to follow the lines of force and rises

30 ELECTRIC TOY MAKING.

along the line of an arc are gradually reaching the position shown.

With a strong magnet and a little bar of steel, con-

FIG. 8. MAHOMET'S COFFIN.

tained in a miniature coffin, the last resting place of the prophet could be well simulated.

Magnetic Jack-Straws.

Magnetic jack-straws are an interesting modification of the time-honored game. They are made up of a set of jack-straws to each of which a piece of iron is attached. They may be given the usual shapes exactly as in the regular game.

In place of the hook there is substituted a magnet. With this the straws are drawn out one by one.

FIG. 9. MAGNETIC JACK-STRAWS.

In the cut a simple way of making the straws is shown. Short pieces of iron or steel wire are used. Some have little blocks of wood fastened to them; others are bent and twisted, others are plain. Different values are assigned to each kind. Each player draws out straws until he shakes or moves one which he is not attempting to remove. He then resigns to the other player. This is kept up until all are withdrawn. The one getting the highest score, as determined by adding up the value of the straws captured, is the winner.

The Magnetic Top.

This amusing toy is easily made. A bar of steel, suitable for the spindle of such a top as shown, is sharpened at one end, and a metallic or heavy wooden disc is fitted to it. The best method of attachment would be by screwing, or by a couple of nuts, one above and one below the disc, the spindle being threaded in either case. The combination is a top. Before putting it together the spindle is magnetized. All shaping, cutting or filing must precede the magnetizing.

FIG. 10. THE MAGNETIC TOP.

A supply of short pieces of iron wire is required; some of these are bent into different shapes, circles, letter S's, etc; others are straight. When the top is spun by the fingers, and one of the wires is placed on the table against its point, it is slowly carried back and forth in the most curious way. It is well, to make it appear still more mysterious, to use cotton or silk covered wire.

As the top rotates, the wire is carried by a sort of friction-pulley action along in the direction of its length. As its end reaches the point of the top it changes sides and returns as it is acted on by the other side of the spindle, and thus goes back and forth, first on one side and then on the other side of the top as long as it spins.

The Magnetic Pendulum.

A universal joint is one that admits of movement in all directions. The construction of a perfect joint of this description is far from a simple matter.

The magnetic pendulum shows how a magnet can be instrumental in producing one.

The original idea of the apparatus was to show the rotation of the earth by Foucault's well-known experiment. A pendulum has fitted to the upper end of its rod, a piece of iron with smoothly rounded upper end. This is suspended from a magnet by simple attraction. Such a pendulum is free to swing

THE MAGNETIC PENDULUM. 33

in any or all planes without being restrained by torsion.

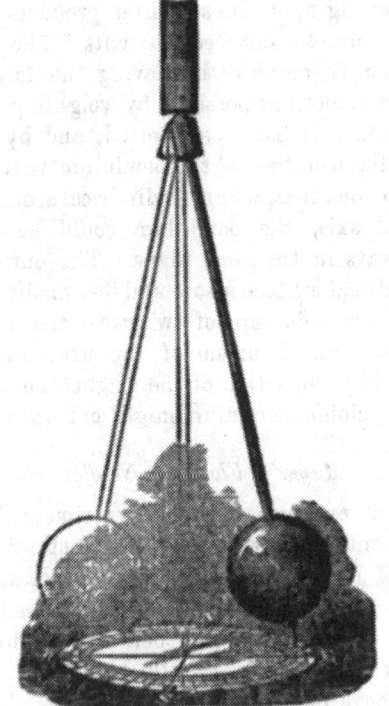

Fig. 11. The Magnetic Pendulum.

It is therefore peculiarly well adapted to be used in proving, by its change of plane of oscillation, the rotation of the earth upon its axis.

It is not to be supposed that the motion is without retardation from its method of suspension. The magnet acting upon the soft iron produces a damping action due to induced currents. The ordinary friction can be reduced by having the face of the magnet as smooth as possible, by weighting the pendulum until it is barely supported, and by accurate finish of the iron top of the pendulum rod.

It is obvious that, using a cylindrical armature with horizontal axis, the pendulum could be made to swing always in the same plane. The curvature of the cylindrical surface also could be modified so as to give a cycloidal arc of swing to the pendulum bob. But the isochronism of the pendulum would be affected by the action of the magnet on the iron, so that a cycloidal pendulum might not prove isochronous.

Mayer's Floating Needles.

This is an exceedingly pretty experiment, being an improvement on the well-known magnetic fishes. A number of large needles are magnetized, all in the same sense as regards their relation of poles to points or eyes. Each needle is then thrust through a small cork, so that only a little bit of the eye end projects above one surface of the corks. They are then floated in a vessel of water as shown, the like poles coming above the surface. Under the effect of repulsion and attraction, they float into the most symmetrical shapes, some of which are shown in the lower diagrams of the cut. To cause them to separate, a magnet pole of the same name as that of their upper ends may be brought above them. This repels them in all directions.

FIG 12 MAYER'S MAGNETIC NEEDLES.

These floating needles are due to Prof. A. M. Mayer, of the Stevens Institute, N. J., and will well repay investigation.

Magnetic Fishes and the Magnetic Swan, Boat, etc.

A few words are enough to describe these well-known toys. The fishes or other objects are made of thin block tin or other non-magnetic material, so as to float in water. Bits of iron or of magnetized steel are secured to them in the proper places. Thus, for the fish, a little bit of iron wire projecting from the mouth is proper. For the swan or boat a piece of magnetized steel may be secured in a similar position.

By a common magnet attached to a thread with a little stick or rod, the fish may be caught. The swan and boat may be attracted or repelled by one or the other poles of the magnet.

By using fish to which different values are assigned, or by having the number stamped upon them in a concealed place, a game can be made up. Each player should catch one fish at a time, alternating with the others. The one who catches those aggregating the largest number would be winner. The numbers of the fish should be concealed, so as to be visible only when out of the water. Thus each player would have to rely on chance for his score.

CHAPTER III.

ELECTRO-MAGNETS.

CONSTRUCTION OF ELECTRO-MAGNETS—MAGNETIZING COILS — THE MAGIC CIRCLE — MAGNETIC HEMISPHERES.

Construction of Electro-Magnets.

ELECTRO-MAGNETS are almost universally made of the horseshoe type. The core should be, for simple sustaining power, thick and short. The cuts through the book show the regulation shapes which curiously enough are not the most powerful. The core is very conveniently made in three pieces, the two arms being tapped or pinned into the yoke. A simple piece of bent **iron**, as shown in the electro-magnet in Figure 5, will suffice for the full core. It must be bent into U shape while hot, if of large size.

The coils may be wound directly on the core, in which case it is well to wrap the latter with paper. Either insulated or bare wire can be used. If the latter, rigorous care must be taken not to permit contiguous windings or coils to touch each other, and a

38   ELECTRIC TOY MAKING.

wrapping of shellacked paper must be employed between each layer of the windings.

On the whole insulated wire is to be recommended. A common mistake is to wind too much wire around the legs. The proper amount and size is a matter of calculation, all depending upon the battery to be employed, and the length and section of the core and its material.

The windings upon both legs must be in opposite directions. After winding the straight portion of one, the wire may be carried diagonally across the intervening space to the opposite face of the other leg, and the winding may thus be continued.

The coils may be made separate as will be described, or may be wound upon bobbins and thrust on as required.

Nothing is gained in general by carrying the windings around the bend.

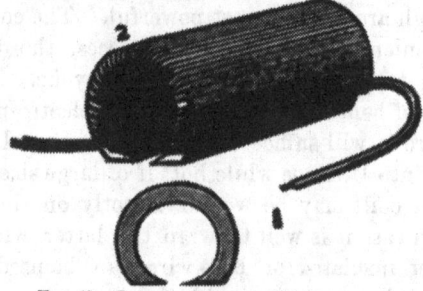

FIG. 13. JOULE'S ELECTRO-MAGNET.

A very powerful form of magnet is here illustrated.

SOLENOID MAGNETS.

It was devised by Joule, largely on experimental bases, and presents an excellent example of a highly efficient electro-magnet.

The core is readily made by filing off one side of a piece of gas pipe. No. 1 shows the section of the core, and No. 2 shows the complete magnet. Here it will be observed the winding is carried around the bend.

Electro-magnets are used in motors, dynamos and bells, and form a very important element in electric constructions. Their power depends on the current which passes around them and on the number of turns of wire through which the current passes. The lifting power in other words is proportional to the ampere turns.

Sometimes a straight bar is used as the core, and sometimes the armature is dispensed with, and the drawing into place of the movable core by the fixed coil, or the drawing of the coil by the fixed core is utilized. Thus, if through a coil of wire a sufficiently intense current is passed, a bar of iron brought into or near the opening of the coil will be drawn or sucked in like a plunger into a cylinder.

The latter type of magnet is ordinarily termed a solenoid, not very correctly however. It was used extensively by Dr. Page in his motors in the early days of the science. It is said that very powerful solenoid magnets were exhibited by the old-time lecturers, some sustaining the weight of several men.

Any magnetizing coil with a bar of iron may be used to illustrate this action. The drawing up of a bar from the table into its axis presents an extraordinary appearance when first seen. It is obvious that another version of Mahomet's coffin could be built upon this, the core being held down by a fine thread. This could be made to present the appearance of a metal bar floating, balloon fashion, at the end of a thread.

The winding of a magnet may be secured in place by glue or varnish, as will be described under "Magnetizing Coils" more fully. It is enough to wind on all the wire and then apply glue to the finished coil, drying, baking, and varnishing or painting.

It is obvious that, if a single length of wire is used for winding, and if the legs are wound separately, one end will come next to the core, and the other end will be on the outside of the wire coils and on the other leg. If wound separately on each leg and afterwards joined across the bend, the ends of the wire may be made to come out symmetrically. As regards appearance it is preferable to have them lie next the iron core; for ease of repair they should be on the outside. The latter is to be recommended.

Magnetizing Coils.

The construction of magnetizing coils, which have no core to support or carry the wire, and in which the wire must be compact and adherent, layer to layer, requires special care. They are wound upon a mandrel, a cylinder generally, which is afterwards withdrawn. It is necessary to arrange so that this withdrawal will be possible; therefore, the mandrel should be slightly tapered, if possible, to facilitate the removal. A glass bottle, a tumbler, or a round ruler or piece of curtain roller are good examples of mandrels.

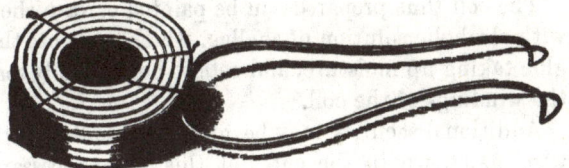

Fig. 14. MAGNETIZING COIL.

To make a magnetizing coil a mandrel of any convenient material is selected. A piece of paper is wrapped around it and on this the insulated wire is wound as neatly as possible. This may be done by hand as regularly as is possible on a lathe, although the use of the latter saves time. Where there are a great number of turns of wire an extemporized winder can easily be put together in a few minutes, the mandrel being used as axle, with a crank handle attached to one end, and then mounted in a couple of standards.

The windings of the coil have to be fastened together. For this purpose carpenters' glue may be employed. The glue is applied to each layer as it is wound and when the last layer is in place the free end of the wire is kept strained until the glue has hardened, which should be in an hour. The whole can then be slipped off the mandrel and dried over a stove.

If, on drying it, the surface shows cracks, they can be stopped up by a further coating of glue, followed by drying.

The coil thus prepared can be painted or varnished with alcoholic solution of shellac, which prevents the glue taking up moisture, and acts to hermetically seal the windings of the coil.

Additional security may be given by binding with wire, as shown in the cut, but this is unnecessary either when glue is employed or when the next described method is adopted.

A much nicer and more effectual way is to use a solution of gum copal in ether. This is applied to layer after layer and solidifies the whole mass with a water repelling medium. Alcoholic solution of shellac can be used in the same way. Heating may be necessary, as in the use of glue, to bring about the last degree of solidification.

The Magic Circle.

The magic circle next illustrated is designed for use with a small magnetizing coil. It is simply two semi-circles of soft annealed iron, provided with rings or handles exactly at the centre of each piece. The

THE MAGIC CIRCLE.

faces are planed or filed off so as to fit accurately. A good size is made of one inch round iron, bent into a circle of three inches internal diameter. For such a circle a coil of number eighteen to twenty wire, wound

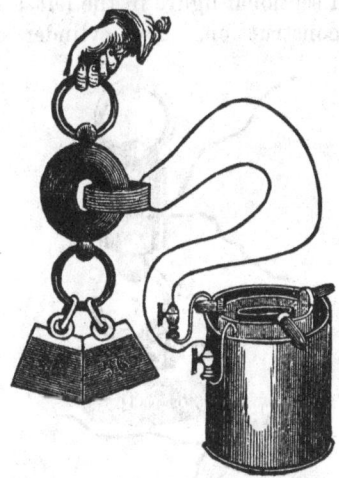

Fig. 15. THE MAGIC CIRCLE.

into forty or fifty turns, suffices. With a current of good strength the attraction the circles will develop is surprising.

Magnetic Hemispheres.

A very peculiar form of magnet is shown in the next cut. Although a modification of it is attributed to Prof. Forbes, by Thompson in his recent work on

44   ELECTRIC TOY MAKING.

the electro-magnet, it is really a very old form. The cut is a reproduction from Davis' Manual of Magnetism, a work copyrighted in 1847. It may aptly be termed the Magdeburgh Hemispheres of Electricity.

The small sectional figure in the left lower corner shows the construction. Two cylinders of soft iron

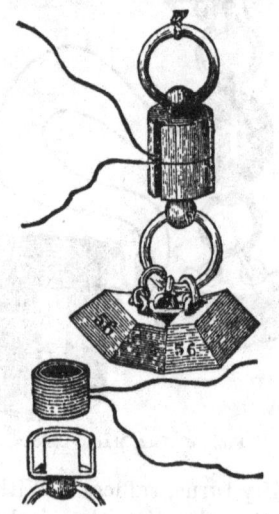

FIG. 16. THE MAGNETIC HEMISPHERES.

have cut out an annular groove of size adapted to receive a magnetizing coil. A slot is cut to permit the wires to come out where the two halves are face to face and in contact.

When the current is turned on and passes through

MAGNETIC HEMISPHERES.

the coil, embedded in the recess, it polarizes the two coils, and if placed together they are strongly attracted. No magnetic circuit, it will be observed, is formed.

The coil may be a movable one, or may be cemented in place with varnish or sealing-wax. Rings should be fitted to both parts. Two persons may be placed in opposition to each other to try to pull them apart. The same magnetizing coil may be used for these as for the magic circle. The metal of the core may be a little heavier than that shown in the cut. These show very little residual magnetism and fall apart easily when the current ceases. The magic circle, on the other hand, retains much residual magnetism even when the current is turned off.

When two people pull against each other in their endeavors to draw apart the halves of this apparatus a sudden breaking of the circuit will cause a sudden giving away or perhaps a fall backwards.

The residual magnetism of the magic circle is so great that to obtain the same sudden separation a reversal of the direction of the current is necessary. This reversal can be easily made by shifting the ends of the wire by hand so as to connect with the other poles of the battery.

CHAPTER IV.

Electric Motors.

PENDULUM COIL MOTOR—RECORDON MAGNET MOTOR—MULTIPOLAR MOTOR—PAGE'S ROTATING ARMATURE—THE ELECTRIC LOCOMOTIVE.

Pendulum Coil Motor.

A VERY pretty form of slow speed motor is shown in the cut, from which the general features of construction can be readily understood. A permanent horseshoe magnet is the basis of construction. This is attached to a board, as shown, so as to be held an inch or so above its surface.

A standard rises from the board just at the end of the magnet. It carries a horizontal axis on which two coils, such as described under magnetizing coils, swing at the end of short bars. These coils encircle the ends of the magnet. A fly-wheel is carried by two other standards and is connected by pitmen with suspension rods of the coils.

The coils are thus connected with the terminals or binding-screws seen on the base.

One terminal connects by the standard and magnet itself with the axis of the fly-wheel. A projecting

PENDULUM COIL MOTOR. 47

segment is attached to this axle, which extends about one-third around the shaft. The two springs seen rising from the base press alternately upon this as the wheel rotates.

From each spring a wire is carried up the large standard and down one of the vibrating rods to a coil. Each coil has its own spring. The other ends

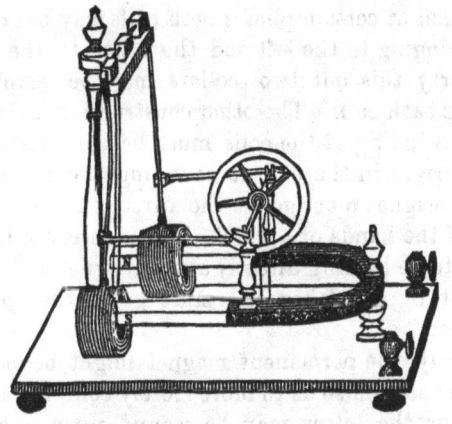

FIG. 17. PENDULUM COIL MOTOR.

of the coils unite and pass down the same standard to the other binding post.

Thus the current entering at one binding post passes by way of the magnet, standards, and fly-wheel axle. The collar is almost always in contact with one spring. The current passes through this, through one of the coils, and leaves it to go to the other binding post, and thence to the battery again. The coil is attracted towards the magnet pole, and as it is drawn thither causes the wheel to rotate. As it reaches the pole and swings beyond it the collar breaks the connection and excites the other coil now most removed from its pole. This is in turn attracted, keeping up the rotation of the wheel. It is also clear that at certain phases both coils may be excited, one swinging to the left and the other to the right. To carry this out two collars may be employed, one for each coil. The other construction is simpler.

The winding of the coils must be thus arranged: The current in the coil surrounding the north pole of the magnet must go in the direction contrary to that of the hands of a watch, if the observer is supposed to be looking directly at the magnet end. The current in the other coil must go in the opposite direction.

Finally, the permanent magnet might be made of circular section so as to more closely conform to the coils, or the latter may be wound upon a square mandrel. In all such constructions it is important to keep the coils near to the field.

This motor illustrates one of the solenoid constructions already alluded to, where the core is stationary and the coils move. It is further to be noted that two round cores of unmagnetized iron can be used instead of a magnet. In such case the direction

Recordon Magnet Motor.

A very neat motor is based upon the same type of magnet as that used in the induction coil shown on a later page. In the present illustration B represents such a magnet, mounted in a frame and provided

FIG. 18. RECORDON MAGNET MOTOR.

with two pole pieces, one projecting from each end. The one on the right has hinged to it the armature A. The other pole piece, E, is so shaped as to admit of the armature going within it, and making as close a fit as compatible with the absence of actual contact. An axle with fly-wheel is journaled in the lower part of the frame. On the axle are a couple of commutator drums, on which two springs, *b b*, press.

The two commutators are of insulating material, wood or ebonite, and one half of the face of each is coated with a slip of brass, which connects with the axle.

One of the binding screws, by a short piece of wire, connects with the frame of the apparatus, with the axle of the fly-wheel and with the metallic commutator sectors. The other binding post connects with one of the coil terminals. The two springs are insulated from the frame, which is effected by using a bar of wood to attach them to. A wire soldered to the screws which attach the springs thereto, runs back of the wood to the other coil terminal. The wire must be insulated from the frame. A pitman is attached to the free end of the armature, and its other end receives the crank pin of a crank fastened to the fly-wheel axle. As the axle rotates the armature will rise and fall, and, as the armature is drawn up and down, the fly-wheel will rotate.

The commutators are so adjusted that when the armature is at its highest point the springs are just in contact with the edge of the metallic segment. This closes the circuit and the armature is attracted and, as it descends, it turns the crank, axle and fly-wheel. It is clear that if the crank turns the wrong way the circuit will at once be broken. For this reason the wheel should be started in the right direction by hand. The armature is therefore drawn down by the magnet as long as contact of springs and commutator sectors last. This ceases just as the armature reaches its lowest point. The momentum of the fly-wheel completes the other half of the revolution, and again closes the circuit through the commutator just as the highest point is reached by the armature.

The same is repeated over and over again, and the wheel is kept rotating as if by a single acting engine.

It is in some respects well to set the commutator so that connection will be made only after the armature has descended a very short distance. This will make the motor less apt to start in the wrong direction.

The extension of the pole pieces gives the magnet a long range of action. The shape is also very compact, and the motor suggests possibilities in the way of improvement. The armature might be wound with wire and thus be excited also so as to increase the attraction.

M. Recordon, it is to be noted, makes these magnets with hollow cores. The aperture can be seen in the cut just back of the left-hand pole piece.

Multipolar Motor.

One of the principal points of merit in a well designed motor is the absence of dead points. The multipolar motor shown in the next illustration,

52   ELECTRIC TOY MAKING.

while it has such, on account of their being subdivided into six for each revolution, is very constant in its movement.

The annular frame, A, and base, F, must be made of

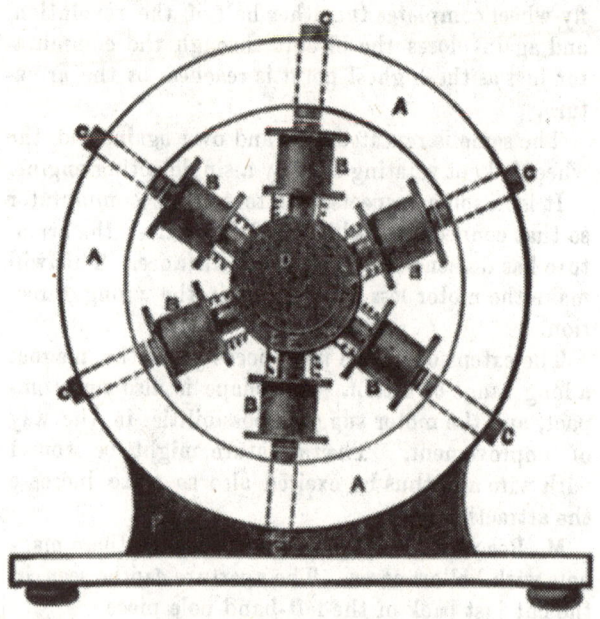

Fig. 19. Multipolar Motor.

some non-magnetic material, such as brass or wood. Through the frame, at even distances, six bars, C, C, of iron are thrust.

These constitute armatures. The rotating field is

MULTIPOLAR MOTOR.

built upon a drum, D, which carries six equally spaced radiating cores, carrying coils of wire, B, B. D may be made of brass or even of wood. A non-conducting or insulating collar, E, surrounds one part of it. The latter collar, E, is designed to receive upon i s surface one set of terminal wires from the magnetizing coils; the other terminals go to the surface of the drum, D.

The magnetizing coils are wound very solidly with insulated wire upon the six cores. They may be further secured by flanges pinned or screwed in place, as the centrifugal force will be considerable.

The connections of the six field magnets are arranged to carry out this principle. During one-half of the total time of a rotation they must be receiving current, but this again must be divided into six periods, which amounts to saying that they are to be excited during alternate twelfths of each revolution. When in the position shown in the cut they are not excited. After they rotate until one-twelfth of a revolution is accomplished, the magnet cores are half way between the outer cores or armatures. At this point they are excited and the current continues for the next twelfth of a revolution, to cease again as the magnets pass the armatures. This is kept up all around the circle.

The six wires carried to the collar, E, connect with a brass or copper ferrule thereon. Six wires or ribs soldered to the ferrule at equal distances apart lie upon the surface of the collar. A copper spring rising from the base presses upon these. The proportions are so adjusted that the spring presses upon each wire during one-twelfth of a revolution. This contact period must correspond to the period when the magnets pass from the central point between armatures to the point opposite the same.

The other six wires run to a ferrule upon the drum D. A second spring presses continually upon this ferrule.

The wires from the battery, or other source of current, connect with the two springs, one wire with each.

If the arrangement thus described is studied it will be seen that the current passes during contact of the spring with the ribs upon the collar, E, or during the proper portions of the revolution. The magnets are all simultaneously excited in parallel, and are attracted to the cores in advance, referred to the direction of their motion. As soon as they reach them the current ceases and their inertia carries them through the next sixth of a revolution, when they are again excited.

The speed such a motor will attain is very great, and hence special care has to be taken to guard against centrifugal force displacing the coils.

Any number of magnets may be employed with a corresponding number of armatures and commutator connections, as the ribs are termed. It will be found

COMMUTATOR FOR MULTIPOLAR MOTOR. 55

that the height as well as breadth of the ribs is a factor in determining the period of contact. The more elegant way is to make each rib exactly one-sixth the circle in width and fill the space between the ribs with insulating material flush with the surface of the ribs, so as to form a true cylindrical surface for the spring to bear against.

The next cut shows in general the plan of connection, only for seven instead of for six magnets. At M is

FIG 20. COMMUTATOR OF MULTIPOLAR MOTOR.

the ferrule upon the drum, against which one spring, C, is constantly pressing. F, F, represent the ribs connected to the collar, against which ribs the other spring, D, bears. Their degree of projection, it will be seen, determines the time of contact. P and N are the wires from the battery, and B is the baseboard. The dotted lines, H, H, indicate the course of two of the wires running to and connected with the ferrule, M.

A modification of this motor should be here alluded to. The magnets are made stationary and occupy the position of the armature bars, while the rotating portion carries only the six armature bars. The commutator bars, springs, and ferrules are identical. One set of terminal wires from the magnets are united and a single larger wire is carried to a binding post. The other ends, in like manner, connect with one of the springs. The other spring connects to the other binding post. Or all the ends of the magnet wires, except those of any two magnets next to each other, may be connected so as to bring the magnets in series. The two free ends are connected as described, by means of the springs, one to the commutator, or ferrule, and the other to the binding post.

Page's Rotating Armature.

A simple form of motor, which may attain very high speed, is shown in the cut. The great velocity of an electric motor is not to be considered an advantage, as it necessitates a reduction of speed by belts and pulleys, or their equivalent.

Upon a fixed base, a permanent U-shaped magnet, N, S, is secured, above which a horizontal fixed piece is supported, forming the top member of a suitable frame. A set-screw, with a conical hole in its end, passes through the centre of this piece. A support, corresponding to the set-screw, is secured to the base directly below it, as shown. This support is a pin with a conical hole drilled in its top. Between the two coned supports a vertical spindle is carried. By

PAGE'S ROTATING ARMATURE.

the set-screw the adjustment can be carried out, so as to leave the spindle free to turn, yet without any end shake.

To the spindle is attached a heavy bar of iron, wound with insulated wire, which is virtually a U-shaped

Fig. 21 Page's Rotating Armature.

electro-magnet. The wire is all wound in the same direction. The ends of the wire are carried to two divisions, *i h*, of a two-part commutator, which is attached to the spindle directly above the rotating magnet, or polarized armature, as it might be called.

Two springs, $g, f,$ of copper, brass, or silver, press against the commutator. Each spring is attached to the frame, and each has its own binding post to receive the wires of the actuating circuit. When the current passes the armature and spindle rotate.

While the construction of the commutator is clear from the perspective view, a small sectional representation is also given. In it A is the section of the vertical spindle. S, S are the two parts of the commutator. They consist of bent plates of copper, or brass, or silver, which are insulated from the spindle. This insulation may be simply a perforated bit of wood to which the plates are cemented by sealing-wax, with a winding of silk at the ends of the plates to further secure them. The plates must of course not touch each other, and are arranged with the two separations almost in the plane at right angles to the plane of the electro-magnet. In the diagram, W, W represent the springs.

FIG. 22 TWO-PART COMMUTATOR.

The general action of the motor is the following: The current, entering by the binding posts and springs through the commutator, magnetizes the core of the electro-magnet, which is generally denominated the armature. The magnetization is such that it is attracted in one direction or the other, assuming that the bar does not lie in the plane of the magnet. Yielding to the attraction it turns on its axis and swings past the poles. As it does this, each spring presses on the other leaf or plate of the commutator. This causes a current, the reverse of the preceding, to pass through the coil, and the bar is at once repelled. As its momentum has carried it past the poles of the magnet it continues its rotation, and is attracted by the distant as well as repelled by the nearer poles. The same action of reversal occurs twice in each revolution.

If the armature lies in the plane of the fixed magnet the motor will not start, but a touch of the finger will suffice to set it going.

The name given to this apparatus is that of the celebrated Dr. Page, who, about half a century ago, endeavored to introduce electric motors. As he had no cheap source of current his work was a failure. If the armature in this motor is turned by power it will generate a current; in other words, the mechanism is reversible.

The Electric Locomotive.

An electric locomotive, based on the use of a motor such as already described under the title of "Page's Rotating Armature" (page 56), is illustrated here. The general construction is clear from inspection of the elevation. The motor is carried horizontally on a little car moving on a railway, and a prolongation of its shaft has on it a worm which gears into a

60 *ELECTRIC TOY MAKING.*

worm-wheel on the axle of one pair of wheels. This pair of wheels is attached rigidly to the axle and constitute the drivers.

Fig. 23 The Electric Locomotive

The current is taken from the rails, the motor acting as a bridge across them. The necessary connections for carrying out the plan, and the arrangements for automatically reversing the engine, will be understood from the view showing the bottom of the platform, the wheels and reversing blocks.

ELECTRIC LOCOMOTIVE. 61

One pair of wheels, those on the left, are mounted loosely, the axle not rotating. The central or darkly shaded part, M, of the axle, is of wood. A wire from the metallic end of the axle, on which the wheel, K, rotates, runs to a central plate, and thence to a plate, G, which plates are insulated. Near G are two plates, E and F, also insulated, except that from each of them a commutator spring, to supply current to the motor, rises.

It is unnecessary to describe the springs and commutator. They are identical with those already described and illustrated (pages 56 to 59).

An insulated switch, A, turns about the central point between E and F. To its pivot, also insulated, a wire is attached, which connects with the journal of the car-wheel, J. The other car-wheel on the same axle is insulated from it by a wooden or vulcanite piece at L.

To the switch pivot a stiff wire with contact piece, C, is soldered. This presses upon E or F, according to the way the switch handle is turned. To the switch handle a second wire is soldered, which is bent so as to bring its two contact pieces, B and D, into the relations shown.

Both these wires must be of spring temper to ensure electrical contact by pressure between their ends and the plates over which they slide.

The moving of the switch handle towards the part corresponding to the lower portion of the cut would shift the contact pieces, B and C, to the reverse position, as regards the plates E and F. C would be shifted to E, and B would be shifted to F; while D would slide along its plate, G, it would not leave it.

As the switch is shown in the cut the current would enter by the wheel, K. It would pass to the plate, G, thence to the plate, E. It would then go through the coil of the armature of the motor, and, leaving it, would go through the plate, F, contact piece, C, switch journal, and its connection to the journal of the wheel, J, and through that wheel to the other rail.

This causes the motor to rotate and propels the car along the track always in the same direction.

Now, if the switch is turned, as already described, so as to reverse the position of the contact pieces, C and B, this will reverse the direction of the current as it goes through the motor, and will reverse the direction in which the car travels.

This reversal may be automatically effected by switch blocks attached to the roadway, two of which are indicated in the plan by H and I. If such are to be used a pin is inserted in the end of the switch, A, shown in the plan and elevation, which strikes the inclined edge of the switch-blocks and shifts over the switch. In an instant the motor is brought to rest and then starts back reversed.

The battery connections are shown in the eleva-

LOCOMOTIVE SWITCH CONNECTIONS. 63

FIG. 24. CONNECTIONS OF RAILS AND ELECTRIC LOCOMOTIVES

tion. The rails must be continuous, or must have their abutting ends connected by plates or wires. The two lines of rail must be well insulated from each other.

Any motor may be used to drive an electric locomotive. The advantage of those working with a permanent magnet for field is that they have a fixed direction of movement.

The elevation shows several details not needing description, such as the set-screws for adjusting the end play of the armature axle.

The general system of reversing might be applied to any other fixed direction motor. One advantage of the automatic reversing is that it obviates the necessity of a circular or continuous track. An improvement would also be to start a short up-grade directly beyond the reversing block to aid in stopping and starting back the motor.

CHAPTER V.

Electric Bells.

THE TOLLING BELL—THE VIBRATING BELL—THE SAFE PROTECTOR.

The Tolling Bell.

ELECTRIC bells are generally of the gong type, and produce a sharp ring. The cut shows how a large regulation-shape bell can be made to toll by an electric current. In many cases the use of a gong would be disagreeable from its sound or appearance. In the arrangement illustrated, the ringing apparatus is all contained within the cavity of the bell so as to be pretty well hidden from sight.

The magnet consists of a perforated iron bobbin with heavy end flanges, of the Recordon type. A couple of pole pieces may be attached to the ends as shown. The magnet is attached to the base of the bell. One of its terminal wires runs through the axis of the extension of the magnet core to the outside of the bell, being insulated from the metal. This obviates the necessity of drilling a special hole in the bell, and possibly impairing its tone. The other terminal wire connects directly with the metal of the bell. A rod, bent into an irregular U shape, carries

66 *ELECTRIC TOY MAKING.*

at one end an iron ball, and constitutes the clapper. To the other limb of the rod a flat-faced bar of iron, long enough to reach from outside to outside of the pole pieces, is fastened. This acts as armature.

The bent bar is pivoted near its centre, as shown.

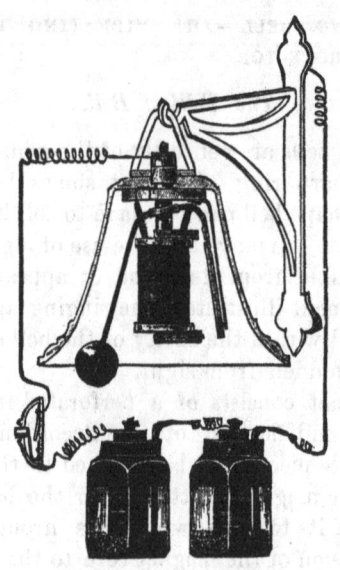

Fig. 25. The Tolling Bell.

A circle or ring is comprised within it at the top of the bend, which opening contains the suspension rod or core extension of the magnet. One pin goes through both sides of the ring and the suspension rod in

THE TOLLING BELL. 67

question. This acts as a very excellent pivoting, preventing lateral shake.

The bell is hung to a metallic bracket. From the battery one wire runs directly to the bracket. It thus connects with the magnet coil, through the metal of the bracket and bell.

The other wire from the battery runs to a key, whence another wire connects with the magnet terminal wire coming out of the bell spindle.

The key may be of the simplest construction, as shown in the cut. When it is depressed, thus closing the circuit, the magnet is excited, attracts its armature and rings the bell.

The peculiar form of the magnet is not only advantageous in compactness of shape but is also supposed to give better results than usual in the way of attractive power.

The Vibrating Bell.

The continuously ringing bell is one which will automatically ring as long as the current continues. It is really a motor. A simple form is shown in the cut.

To a base-board is attached an electro-magnet. A bar of soft iron, which is its armature, is carried by a flat spring which draws it away from the magnet. A contact screw is so arranged as to touch the armature spring when the armature is drawn away from the magnet. To the armature is attached a wire,

68 *ELECTRIC TOY MAKING.*

carrying a ball, which serves as a clapper. A gong is fastened by its central post to the same base-board, which also may carry two binding posts.

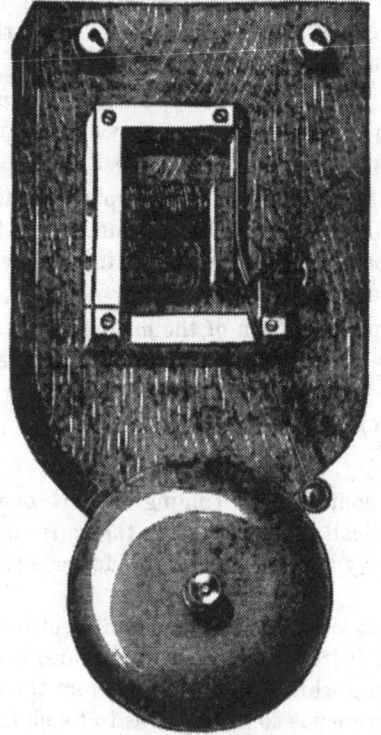

Fig. 26. The Vibrating Bell.

The connections are shown in dotted lines. From

one binding post a wire runs directly to one of the magnet terminals. From the other terminal of the magnet the wire connects with the armature spring. From the other binding post a wire runs to the metallic support of the contact screw.

When no current passes, the armature is drawn back from the bell, and the spring is in contact with the contact screw. If, now, a current is caused to pass, it enters by one of the binding screws and excites the magnet, its course going through the spring and contact screw. The magnet attracts its armature, and opens the circuit by drawing the spring away from the contact screw. The attraction of the armature draws the clapper against the bell and gives a ring. As the circuit is opened the armature springs back and again closes the circuit. Again the armature is attracted and the bell rings. This operation is repeated over and over again as long as the current is kept up.

The usual way of turning on the current is by a press-button, which construction is so simple as to need no description. It is seen in section on the left hand of the cut on page 66. Any form of switch will answer the same purpose.

The Safe Protector.

This apparatus is what may be termed a combined electrical and mechanical safe protector. The illustration shows its application and principle.

In Fig. 2 the ordinary bell, such as described in its

proper place (page 67), with battery, switch-box or "thief detector," and safe are shown. From the safe two wires, I J, are carried to the switch-box. Within the safe is a spring-switch, which, when pressed, maintains an open circuit, and when released

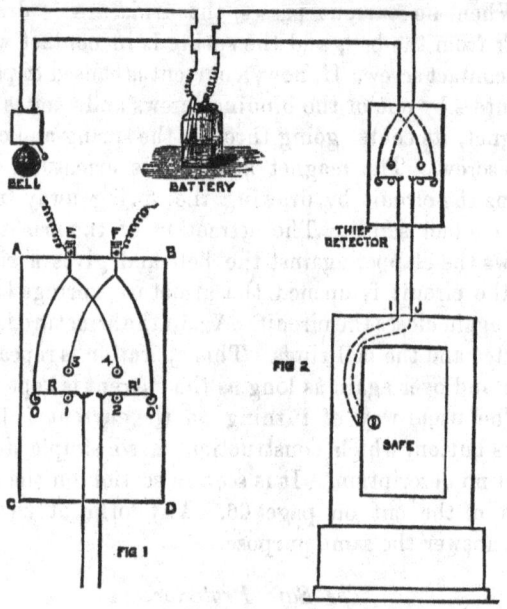

Fig. 27. The Safe Protector.

by the opening of the safe door, closes the circuit. Such a switch is so simple that enlarged description is not required. This switch is actuated by the safe

THE SAFE PROTECTOR.

door. When closed, the door keeps the circuit open by pressing on the switch. When the door is opened the circuit closes, as the switch is released from pressure.

Two wires from the battery and bell circuit lead to the switch-box, connecting with the binding screws, E, F, Fig. 1, on top of the box, A B C D. Within the box each wire bifurcates as shown, and has its two terminals connected to the two pairs of pins, O^1, 3 and O, 4 respectively. On the pins, O, O^1, two springs, R, R^1, work, to whose outer ends the safe wires are attached. These wires draw the springs down until they press against the steady-pins 1 and 2.

If, now, the safe is opened the circuit closes and the bell rings. If the burglar, before opening the safe, noticing the wires, I, J, cuts one of them to secure himself from detection, the spring R or R^1, as the case may be, springs up and makes contact with the stud, 3 or 4, on the opposite bell and battery terminal. This, of course, closes the circuit, also, and the bell rings. The same is the case if both wires are cut. Both springs then fly up and the circuit is closed just as before.

It will, of course, be an object to hide the switch-box, because if one or both of the leads from bell and battery are severed, the apparatus will become inoperative. The wires, I, J, must also be so fixed as to appear like ordinary electric leads. They must be perfectly free for their entire lengths.

ELECTRIC TOY MAKING.

If the burglar understood the construction all he would have to do would be to secure the wires, I J, by staples or by tying, and then to cut them off below the staples. This would prevent the bell from ringing and would enable the safe to be opened. It is assumed, however, that the natural course of cutting one or both of the wires will be followed by any illicit operator, who attempts to prevent the electric alarm from operating.

CHAPTER VI.

Miscellaneous Toys.

THE ELECTRIC DANCER—THE MAGIC DRUM—THE ELECTRIC HAMMER—ELECTRIC INSECTS—THE INCANDESCENT LAMP.

The Electric Dancer.

THIS amusing toy originally was produced to be operated entirely by hand. The electrical modification is based upon the principle of the vibrating bell, and needs but a short description. The cuts show one construction very clearly.

A box contains the motive mechanism. This consists of an electro-magnet with a soft iron armature carried by a spring. A wire from the battery goes directly to the magnet. The other terminal of the magnet connects with the armature spring at L^1. The other end of the spring is bent at right angles at L^2, and carries a platform on a support L^3. This is the dancing platform. A contact spring, S S, is carried by the armature spring. A contact screw, C, is adjustable as regards its contact with the spring S S. From it a wire runs to the binding post, B, to which the other battery wire is attached.

74 ELECTRIC TOY MAKING.

The magnet may have as cores round iron bars ⅝ inch in diameter, 1¼ inch long, and wound to 1⅛ inch diameter, with No. 26 silk covered wire.

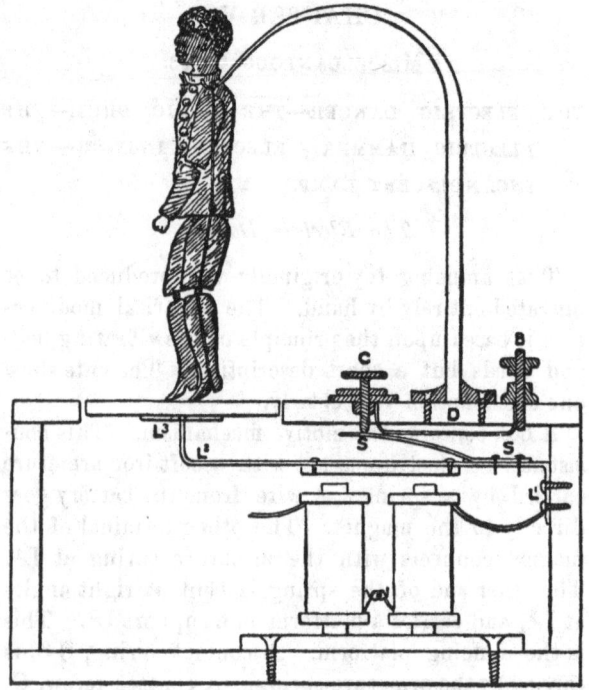

Fig. 28. The Electric Dancer. Elevation.

The action of a current on such mechanism is to keep the platform in constant vibration, which may

THE ELECTRIC DANCER. 75

be regulated and modified over quite a range of action by the screw, C.

The figure is made of wood, with very loose joints, and is suspended by a curved arm, so that its feet

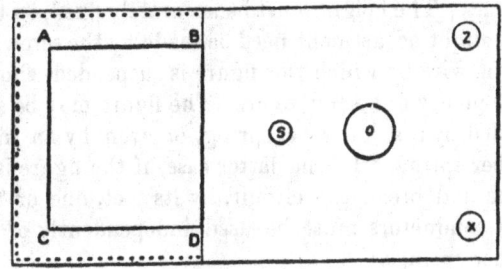

FIG. 29. THE ELECTRIC DANCER. PLAN

just touch the stage. When a current passes, the figure begins to dance, and keeps it up as long as the battery supplies enough energy.

Another way of working it is to make the figure do the making and breaking of the circuit. For this end, the binding post, B, should be connected to the curved suspension-rod, instead of connecting with the contact screw, C. Jointed wires are carried through the figure, and the ends are soldered to light brass, or copper plates, on the soles of the feet. The armature spring is in electrical contact with the top of the dancing platform, which must have a metallic surface. Very thin sheet brass, or copper, may be used for this.

In the last construction, the screw, C, and spring,

S S, may be retained, but there must be no connection between them and the binding post, B.

Thus arranged, the feet will make and break the circuit. The jointed wires of one side are shown in the cut. The height must be accurately fixed, so that only slight adjustment need be made by the screw, C.

The wire by which the figure is suspended, should have plenty of spring to it. The figure may be suspended by a spiral wire spring, or even by an India rubber spring. In the latter case, if the figure is to make and break the circuit, by its feet, one or two wire conductors must be used independently of the rubber springs.

Two or three Leclanché cells will work the figure for a short time—for larger periods a more constant type of generator must be used.

The Magic Drum.

The magic drum has been exhibited by many professional magicians. When it is shown on a stage, far from the eyes of the audience, it can be easily manipulated, with little refinement, as far as concealment of its mode of action is concerned. The trick is doubtless familiar to our readers. A drum is hung, by one or two cords, from the top of the proscenium arch, or ceiling, and, in response to the performer's orders, plays, raps, etc.

The newer construction here illustrated, due to Mr. Geo. M. Hopkins, is superior, as it requires only

THE MAGIC DRUM. 77

one suspending cord, and, without close inspection, it is far from obvious how the result is brought about.

The drum must contain some apparatus for making a sound. As shown in No. 2, the apparatus consists of a magnet and armature, D, both secured firmly

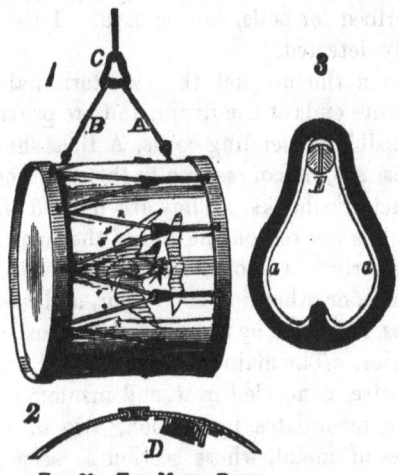

FIG. 30. THE MAGIC DRUM.

to the body of the drum. The armature should be as close to the poles of the magnet as possible, without touching, even when the current is turned on.

A sudden exciting or releasing from excitement of the magnet will produce a sound, on the general principle of the make and break sounds in a telephone.

The advantage of this apparatus is that it can be so small and light as to be impossible of detection by the closest inspection. Placed close to the embouchure of the drum it will fall outside of the line of sight of any one looking into the interior.

If preferred, any form of rapping device, such as described for bells, can be used. These will be more easily detected.

From the magnet the two terminal wires run to opposite ends of the drum, and are provided with two ostensible suspending cords, A B, as shown in No. 1. These are, of course, really the conductors, and end in metallic hooks. They are hooked into a ring, C, which is hooked on the end of the suspending cord.

The ring is shown in detail in No. 3. It is of ebonite, or other non-conductor, and has two metallic strips, indicated by the unshaded areas, $a\ b$, within its interior. The main suspending cord, which includes two wires concealed in it, and insulated, one from the other, terminates in a hook, also of two insulated pieces of metal, whose section is seen at E. Each piece of this hook is connected with one of the two wires in the suspending cord.

It is obvious that, if the drum is suspended as shown, the two wires of the suspending cord may, at their further end, be attached to an electric circuit. If the current is turned on and off, a sound will be produced each time.

The single suspension cord, and the single hook

thereon, with the intermediate ring, and apparent absence of any sounding apparatus within the interior of the drum, enhance the mystery above the ordinary.

The drum may even be passed around for inspection. If this is to be done, it is well to remove the short suspending ends, A B, so that only a couple of rings for hanging it will be visible. In such case, the cords, A, B, should have hooks at both ends.

The Electric Hammer.

This toy, although, if made small, it is only a sort of model of a steam hammer, can be made quite powerful enough to be of some service. For the latter end, it would be well to vary the construction a little, and to use a polarized hammer spindle. Simplicity is favored by the construction described.

As shown in the cut, it comprises a solenoid or deep magnetizing coil, mounted on a suitable frame and base. Under the axis of the core is placed an anvil.

A bar of soft iron nearly fits the opening in the centre of the coil. The lower end of the bar is fitted with an enlargement to represent the hammer head.

One battery wire connects directly with one of the coil terminals. The other battery wire is attached to a flat rubbing plate of ebonite, or hard wood, which is secured by a single screw to the frame, so that it can be swung up or down, as desired. The attachment of the wire thereto is effected by a screw screwed into the plate, and through which its point extends.

80   *ELECTRIC TOY MAKING.*

The point is then filed off so as to be exactly flush with the face of the plate.

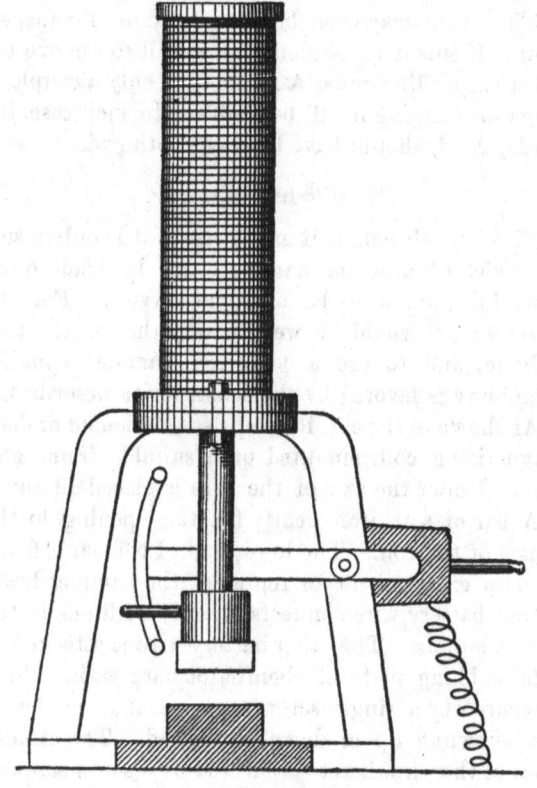

Fig. 31. The Electric Hammer. Elevation.

THE ELECTRIC HAMMER.

The second terminal of the coil is soldered to the metallic frame at any convenient point.

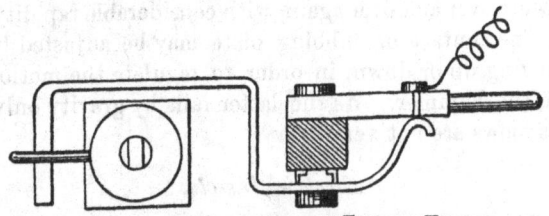

FIG. 32. PLAN OF CONNECTIONS OF ELECTRIC HAMMER.

To the frame a swinging arm is pivoted, the same pivot serving for it and for the contact plate. It is bent so as to pass back of the stem of the hammer, and has two striking pins extending from it. A pin attached to the hammer stem, strikes one of these pieces, as the hammer rises, and another as it falls.

The action of the hammer, when connected to a battery, is as follows: The current passes by the contact screw, vibrating or swinging arm, and frame to the magnet, and leaves it by the regular connection.

The solenoid attracts and draws up the hammer. As it rises, the striking pin encounters the upper projection on the swinging arm, and raising it, displaces its end from the contact pin. This opens the circuit, stops the current, and the hammer falls. As it nearly reaches the anvil the pin again strikes the lower projection on the swinging arm, and, pressing it down, brings its end over the contact screw, thus closing the circuit and again exciting the solenoid. The hammer is lifted and the same succession of movements occurs over and over again, with considerable rapidity.

The contact or rubbing plate may be adjusted by moving up or down, in order to regulate the motion of the hammer. As the latter falls by gravity only, its blows are not very heavy.

Electric Insects.

The base of the interesting toy next described, and due to Mr. Geo. M. Hopkins, is an electro-magnet, which is made to constitute the body of an insect. The first insect to be spoken of is the electric butterfly.

The sectional views of the body show a straight, soft iron core, to which an arched pole piece, h, is attached at the front of the insect's thorax. The back of the butterfly is a thin plate of iron attached to the other end of the core by the screw, g. To this plate two small armatures, $i\,i$, are pivoted at f, as shown, which extend down and over the ends of the pole piece, h. To these armatures the wings are attached. In making these there is room for artistic taste.

The armatures are made so much heavier than the wings that the latter stand erect. It is, however, a simple matter to introduce a fine German silver or brass wire spring to keep the armatures away from the pole piece.

The core is wrapped with No. 24 silk-covered wire,

ELECTRIC INSECTS. 83

and the terminals are made to represent, or are carried through or back of two of the insect's legs. The con-

Fig. 33. Electrical Butterfly.

structor must not forget to put on the head with proper adjuncts.

When a current is passed through the insect the wings will be depressed. They will rise again on being released. The current may be turned on by hand, or an automatic circuit breaker, such as shown in the next cut, may be used.

This consists of a pendulum, whose motion is maintained by electricity. Near its top the rod carries an armature. The lower end of the rod, which must be of metal, and should terminate in a platinum point, passes, in its motion, through a globule of mercury. An electro-magnet is fixed near the armature. The circuit, which includes the butterfly, or several of its kindred, and a battery, n, runs through the current breaker, thus:

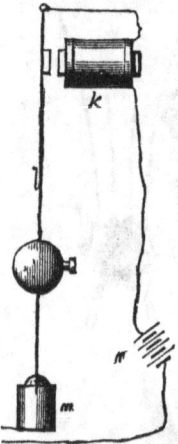

FIG 34. PENDULUM CIRCUIT BREAKER.

One terminal goes to the electro-magnet, k, and thence connects by its suspension bracket, with the pendulum rod; going through this, the current passes through the globule of mercury on m, to the other terminal which is connected therewith.

Thus the butterfly and the pendulum magnet are both excited, and the pendulum is attracted. If the pendulum is started swinging, it will, as it leaves the mercury globule, open the circuit, and the butterfly will move its wings; at the same time the magnet ceases to pull it. It swings back, and as it passes through the globule, is attracted by the magnet as the circuit closes, and the butterfly again moves its wings in the reverse direction.

This can be kept up as long as desired. The exact

ELECTRIC INSECTS. 85

position of the mercury globule, to give a good swing, must be determined by experiment. The plumb-bob

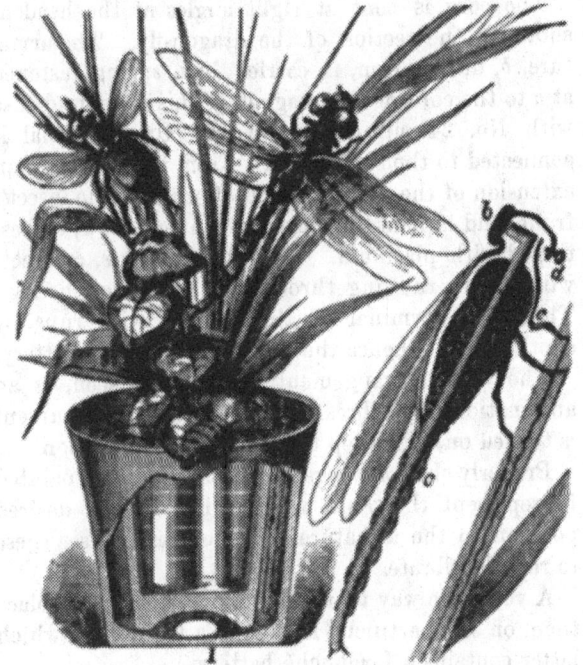

FIG. 35. ELECTRICAL DRAGON-FLY AND BEE

is also made adjustable, so as to allow of varying the time of movement of the insect's wings.

The dragon-fly and bee are more independent. They are by nature quicker in their motions than the butterfly, and are constructed to rapidly move or "buzz" their wings.

The core is bent at right angles at the head as shown in the section of the dragon-fly. The armature, b, of soft iron, is carried by a spring fastened at c to the core of the magnet. This is wound also with No. 24 silk-covered wire. One terminal is connected to the spring at c. From the armature an extension of the spring reaches down over the insect's front, and is bent to receive a contact screw, d, best tipped with platinum. A contact piece, e, connects with a wire running through, or by, one of the legs. The other terminal of the magnet wire runs by another leg. Thence the two are carried to a battery.

The whole arrangement, it will be seen, is an automatic circuit breaker, and as long as the current is turned on, will keep the armature in vibration.

Properly shaped wings made of mica, and painted to represent the veins, are attached in any desired position to the armature. The current causes these to rapidly vibrate.

A very nice way to mount the insects is to place them on some artificial flowers in a flower pot, which latter contains a Leclanché battery.

One of the battery terminals connects with the insect. The other runs to the base of the flower pot. Here it nearly meets one of the terminal wires from the insect. A globule of mercury is so disposed as to leave the circuit open, if all is on a level table. If

THE INCANDESCENT LAMP. 87

lifted, or tipped a little, the mercury shifts and makes contact with both wires, closing the circuit and making the insects start into seeming life.

The Incandescent Lamp.

The amateur should not attempt to make incandescent carbon filament lamps. These are for sale, of all descriptions and sizes. A platinum wire lamp, unregulated, is easily made, and with a carefully regulated current is very good as a toy, but is of little practical value. The end of a test tube may be used to represent the bulb, and a bent loop of fine platinum wire to represent the filament. The ends of the platinum are soldered to two copper wires considerably thicker than themselves. The copper wires are thrust through a cork which closes the end of the tube.

The platinum wire should be fine, No. 28 to 30. The copper wire should be not less than No. 25.

The next cut shows a regulated platinum lamp, which might render real service, although it would never be as efficient as the carbon filament lamp, with its almost perfect vacuum.

A base carries two binding posts and a glass shade or bulb, and the mechanism of the lamp. From the binding posts wires run to a post, B, and a short screw at C. The latter screw holds down against the base a high arched piece. To the post, B, a rocker, A, is pivoted. From the arched piece to the rocker a platinum wire, P, extends.

88　　ELECTRIC TOY MAKING.

As shown in the cut, the current entering by one post passes through the wire and out by the other post. As the wire expands with the heat, the left end of the rocker descends. The adjustment is such that contact is made before the platinum is hot enough

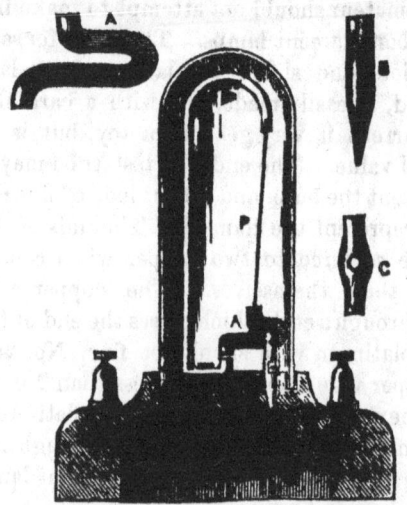

FIG. 36.　SELF-REGULATING PLATINUM LAMP.

to melt. This short circuits the wire, and the heat falls; as the wire contracts, it breaks the contact and again grows hot. These operations in practise succeed each other so rapidly, and are of such slight degree, that all appears perfectly stationary, and no vibration is perceptible.

CHAPTER VII.

Spark and Induction Coils, and Allied Subjects.

THE SPARK COIL—THE INDUCTION COIL—RECORDON'S INDUCTION COIL—THE MAGNETO-GENERATOR—ELECTRIC ARTILLERY—ELECTRIC GYMNASTICS—ANO-KATO—SIMPLE EXPERIMENTS IN STATIC ELECTRICITY.

The Spark Coil.

For the production of a simple spark for lighting gas, firing an explosive mixture, and the like, a spark coil may be employed. It is simpler in construction than an induction coil. It practically represents a single coil, either primary or secondary, of the more complicated apparatus.

To construct one, a core of iron wire is first made. This may be a bundle of pieces of wire of gauge No. 20, or thereabouts. The pieces composing it should be about eight inches long, and the bundle should represent a cylinder about $\frac{3}{4}$ inch in diameter.

A very good plan is to put the pieces of wire in a coal fire in the evening, and to allow them to become red hot. They are left in the fire over night until it has grown cold. This anneals them and leaves them covered with a thin film of oxide. The latter is a non-conductor of electricity, and its presence acts to break up the continuity of the core.

On this the coil is wound. It may be made of No. 20 wire, insulated with cotton. What is sold as magnet wire will answer perfectly. This should be wound on until the whole is about three times the diameter of the core. The wire windings should cover as nearly as possible the whole of the core.

If such a coil is placed in circuit with a battery, the parallel component windings of wire act one upon the other, when the current is turned on or off, and produce a high potential difference. This causes the production of a spark. The spark is strongest when the current is suddenly shut off by breaking the circuit. As the coil is normally on an open circuit, and as the operation of producing a spark consists in suddenly depressing and releasing a key, thus opening and closing the circuit in quick succession, a double spark or discharge is produced.

The battery for operating a spark coil should be, as a general rule, arranged in series. This gives as a starting point the highest attainable potential difference, which again is magnified or increased by the self-induction of the coil.

The tendency of the day is to use coils for high tension effects. Regular induction coils are to be recommended for powerful tension, but where a spark suffices, the spark-coil answers every purpose.

So true is this that, on an emergency, any electro-magnet, such as is used in a telegraph sounder, or for lifting weights, and the like, can be made to do service as a spark-coil. The ready production of a spark on opening a circuit goes to prove that it includes a high potential battery, or that electro-magnets, or some form of coil, are actuated by it.

The Induction Coil.

The induction coil is, in general terms, an apparatus for converting a current of one intensity into a current of a greater or less intensity. Conversely with the change of intensity there is an inverse change in the potential difference of such parts of the circuit as represent the entering and outgoing terminals of the coil. To bring about this change a steady current cannot be directly used—if such is the one to be acted upon it must first be converted into an irregular or varying one. The first, or unconverted current, is called the primary current. The converted current, produced by the action of the coil, is called the secondary current; it is always an interrupted current, and of the type known as alternating.

An induction coil may be very easily constructed. As a toy, for giving shocks and similar uses, it may be quite small. But as the size increases the difficulties of construction increase. The very large coils, giving from twelve to forty-two inch sparks, require the highest skill of the apparatus maker.

For the amateur the induction coil will generally be designed to increase potential difference at the expense of intensity. The illustrations show the features of construction of a simple coil designed to do this.

Before going further it should be understood that nothing absolute can be said of the size of a coil, or of the wire composing it. All this is a matter of calculation, and depends upon the current to be used, and upon the current to be obtained from the coil.

The coil proper of the drawing consists of the core, A, primary coil, B, insulating coating, C, and secondary coil, D. The wires of the secondary coil are kept insulated from the primary, and the greatest care must also be taken to keep the different windings of both secondary and primary insulated from each other.

The core consists of a bundle of iron wires, about No. 18. These are laid together so as to form a cylinder. They may be annealed and oxidized as described for the spark coil. After wrapping the core with some shellacked paper, the primary wire is wound on as compactly as possible. It should be insulated wire, and it is well, if it is cotton covered, to paint over the successive layers with alcoholic solution of shellac.

For ordinary coils No. 18 wire is a good size, and two wrappings around the core may be employed.

A paste-board tube such as used for mailing drawings or papers which are not to be folded, serves to

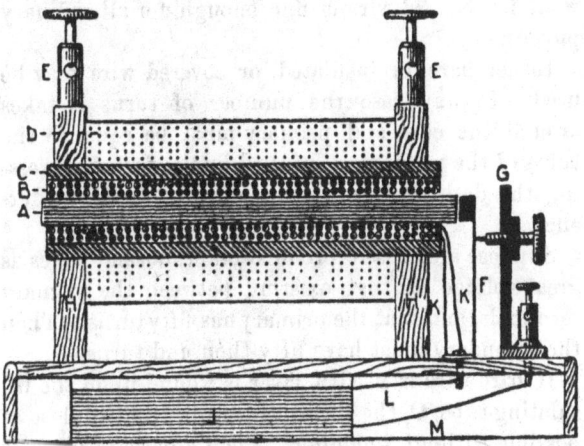

Fig. 37. Induction Coil

cover the primary coil and core. On this the secondary core is wound. The tube must be well paraffined.

Here, far more precautions in the way of insulating the wire have to be taken. The wire itself is much finer. If the potential is to be raised to one thousand times the original difference, the wire will answer if of one-thousandth the section of the primary. Turns enough must then be given to it to ensure this ratio.

As a matter of practise the secondary is often made of coarser wire than is required under the above supposition. Very fine wire is expensive, and is difficult to work, as it is liable to break very easily when being wound. No. 36 wire is fine enough for all ordinary purposes.

Either bare, or insulated, or covered wire may be used. In any case the number of turns it takes around the core and primary must be equal to the turns of the primary multiplied by the factor expressing the desired ratio of increase of potential difference.

Suppose a coil is to produce one thousand times as great voltage as that existing between the primary terminals, and that the primary has fifty turns. Then the secondary must have fifty thousand turns.

If bare wire is used a layer is wound upon the insulating tube, C, the successive turns lying as close as possible without touching. Then a piece of paper is wound over the wire, and is shellacked, and the winding is continued over it. This goes on until the desired number of turns are obtained. As this involves a long piece of winding it is best to do it on the lathe.

An excellent plan is to wind only a half inch in length of the secondary at a time, but to wind each half inch to the full thickness before beginning the next. To execute this, a bit of thin board with a hole the size of the insulating tube in it is needed. This is thrust up to within half an inch of the end of the coil, and the space between it and the end is

THE INDUCTION COIL. 95

wound to the full thickness; then it is shifted half an inch and the winding is thus continued until done.

In any case a temporary flange of some kind is needed at the ends to keep the coils square.

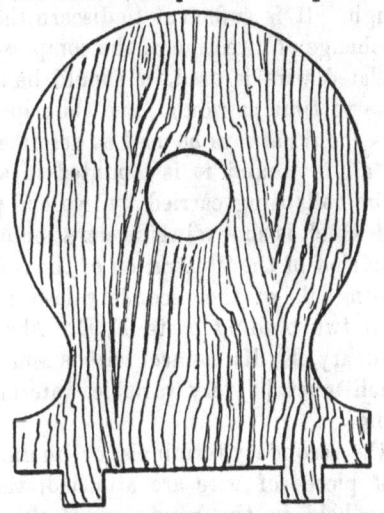

FIG. 38. END PIECE OF FRAME OF INDUCTION COIL.

From time to time the wire should be tested for continuity, as it is very apt to break. If it does part, it may be carefully twisted together, and it is well to solder it. This can be done in the flame of an alcohol lamp. In testing its continuity an ordinary compass can be utilized as the galvanometer. If a dozen turns of the wire are taken around it a slight current will deflect the needle. The compass must be so placed that the coils lie in the magnetic meridian. As battery, a copper coin and a bit of galvanized iron, immersed for the moment in dilute sulphuric acid, will answer if the galvanometer is sensitive enough. It is sufficient to discern the smallest possible change of direction of the compass-needle.

If insulated wire is used, it should be shellacked from time to time as wound, and the paper between the layers should always be used as described.

When all is wound it is mounted in a frame as shown, the coil being carried by two end pieces, H, H, one of which is shown in side elevation on a larger scale than that of the illustration of the coil.

The terminals of the secondary lead to and are soldered to two binding posts, E, E. The terminals of the primary, K, K, connect with a source of current which must be very variable, intermittent, or alternating.

If to the secondary terminals, or binding posts, a couple of pieces of wire are attached, the ends of which are held in the hands, and if then an intermittent current is passed through the primary, a series of shocks will be experienced.

For this purpose it is best to attach handles of brass tubing, about half an inch in diameter, to the ends of the wires, in order to give a larger surface of contact. Wet sponges may, with advantage, be used on the tubing, although as this is not necessary and is rather unpleasant, it is not generally done.

Sparks may also be taken from the coil by bringing the ends of two conductors from the secondary terminals sufficiently close. A very small coil, two or three inches long, will give a one-eighth inch spark, and some of the large ones will give a spark several feet long, one which will pierce a glass plate two inches or more in thickness.

The primary circuit may be broken by hand. One of the old methods consisted in connecting one end of the primary to the battery, and the other to a very

FIG. 39. CIRCUIT BREAKER.

coarse cut file. The teeth of the file might be an eighth of an inch apart, and as high as possible. Then the other wire from the battery was drawn across the file, and, as it jumped from tooth to tooth, effected the desired "make and break."

Another way of doing it by hand is shown in the cut. A cog-wheel from an old clock, or elsewhere, is mounted on a metallic frame, which is in connection with one of the battery wires. A spring wire presses against the teeth as the wheel rotates. This spring is in connection with one of the primary terminals of the coil. The other primary terminal is in direct connection with the battery. Thus the make and break is obtained by turning the wheel.

The coil itself may be made to do the making and breaking. As shown in the cut it is thus arranged: On the base are two binding posts, which are the primary terminals. One of the primary terminal wires, K, K, runs directly to one of the binding posts. The other primary terminal wire runs to the base of the vertical spring, F. At its top this spring carries a block of soft iron which acts as an armature. The other binding post seen in the elevation connects with the metallic standard, G. An adjustable contact screw, with platinum point, goes through the top of the standard. The spring normally presses against this screw. It is well to rivet a little bit of platinum on the spring at the point of contact.

When the terminals from a battery are attached to the binding screws the action is obvious. The spring, F, making contact through G with the battery, closes the primary circuit and a current goes through the

THE INDUCTION COIL. 99

primary. This magnetizes the core and the armature on the spring is attracted. It draws the spring away from the contact screw and breaks the circuit. The core ceases to be magnetic and the spring flies back and renews the contact. This action is kept up as long as connection with the battery is maintained, the makes and breaks succeeding each other with great rapidity.

As thus described, the induction coil is far from perfect. A violent sparking action takes place at the make and break contact and there is considerable waste of energy. Both these bad features can be diminished by the use of a condenser, whose construction will be next explained.

It would consist, in its simplest plan, of two leaves of tin-foil separated from each other, one connected to the spring, F, and the other to the standard, G. The area must be quite large so that as a matter of convenience it is best built up of small pieces of tin-foil laid in a pile that fits the base of the instrument, which is made into a box to contain them. The connections and general features of the condenser are best shown in the plan view.

Each piece of foil is cut with projecting ears, A, B, at one of the corners. The shape is seen in the plan view given here. A piece of paper, saturated with paraffine wax, is placed between each two sheets. In piling up the sheets of tin-foil the ears, A, or B, of each sheet are placed at the opposite corners as

100   *ELECTRIC TOY MAKING.*

indicated in the plan. It is now evident that if the projecting ears are bent down or pressed together, each set of leaves of tin-foil will be insulated from the other, but all the leaves of each set will be in electrical connection with each other. To

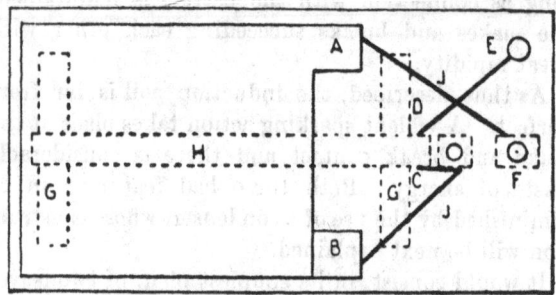

Fig. 40. Plan View of Induction Coil.

ensure all this, the paper should be cut an eighth of an inch longer and wider than the tin-foil. The paper can be easily waxed or paraffined by applying the wax in shavings and melting it with a hot sad-iron, or in an oven or over a stove.

Referring now to the plan, in it E denotes one of the binding posts to which the battery wire is to be connected. H is the primary coil. From E a wire is carried to and connects at D with one of the terminals of H. The other terminal of H, denoted by C, connects with the spring (F, in the elevation), whose base is shown in the plan. The other binding post which, it will be remembered, is in connection with the contact screw post (G, of the elevation), is shown at F in the plan. From this contact screw post a wire connects with one set of tin-foil sheets, A, while from the spring a wire connects with the other set of sheets, B.

The action of the condenser is apparent in the reduction of the size of the spark between the make and break surfaces, and in the lengthening of the other secondary spark. In other words, a condenser greatly improves the action of an induction coil, and should always be used.

As an example of a miniature coil the following data may be given: Core, 4 inches long, and as thick as a lead pencil. Length between end pieces, 3 inches. Primary coil, two ounces of No. 18 wire. The secondary wound to within $\frac{1}{4}$ inch of the insulating tube, with two ounces of No. 36 wire. The condenser, twenty pieces tin-foil, each 3 inches square.

An excellent way of making the insulating tube is to saturate a piece of blotting paper with paraffine wax. A wooden mandrel is wrapped with a piece of writing paper, whose free end is pasted down to the paper. This must be free to slide on and off. The mandrel must be of the diameter of the primary. On this the blotting paper is wound, being pressed into place with a hot iron. This solidifies it by melting the wax. It should be one-twentieth of an inch thick.

The tension of the shocks may be graduated by

pulling the core out or pressing it in. Its removal greatly reduces the intensity of action. Or else a space may be left between the secondary and primary, and a brass tube may be arranged to slide in and out of this space. The removal of the tube increases the energy of action.

Recordon's Induction Coil.

A very good form of induction coil is shown in the next cut which at least possesses the merit of novelty.

Fig. 41. Recordon's Induction Coil.

It is disadvantageous in not admitting the convenient use of a wire core.

The core which is hollow, is made of soft, annealed

RECORDON'S INDUCTION COIL.

iron, turned so as to represent a spool or bobbin with deep flanges at each end. It is mounted as shown, wound with primary and secondary coil, B, as described for the other form of coil. The secondary connects with two binding posts on the base, one of which is seen at N. Of the primary terminals, one connects with the standard, D, the other with the binding post, b. From the binding post, b^1, a wire runs to the standard, C.

To the top of the standard, D, a spring is screwed to which an iron block, A, is attached. The standard, C, carries a contact screw with platinum point. The iron block, A, acts as the armature of the magnet. The piece, P, is simply designed to regulate the period of vibration and prevent too rapid a succession of makes and breaks. The battery connects with the binding posts, b^1 and b.

When the current passes to the primary coil through the standard, C, contact screw, spring and standard, D, it excites the core, which becomes a magnet. The armature, A, is attracted and draws the spring away from the contact screw. This opens the circuit. The core ceases to attract the armature and it springs back. The contact screw again comes in contact with the spring, and the current again passes. Thus the make and break is effected practically as in the case of the other coil.

Although shown without a condenser, it will work far better if it has one.

This coil may be fitted with a regulator. To do this the barrel should be turned down so as to be very thin. It may even be made of sheet iron, bent into a tube and soldered along its seam, and to the heavy flanges. A bundle of iron wires is then arranged to fit into the tube, and to be slid in or out as desired. The more there are within the tube the greater will be the effect of the coil.

The dimensions of the coil illustrated are as follows: Diameter of coil, $3\frac{27}{100}$ inches; thickness of flanges, $\frac{2}{10}$ inch; exterior diameter of core, $1\frac{6}{10}$ inch; interior diameter of flange, $1\frac{4}{10}$ inch; distance between flanges, $1\frac{7}{10}$ inch. Primary wire, $\frac{47}{100}$ lb. avoirdupois No. 18 wire; secondary wire (in 31 layers), $\frac{82}{100}$ lb. avoirdupois No. 32 wire. There is, of course, nothing absolute in these dimensions.

The Magneto-Generator.

A very powerful and compact form of magneto-generator is the subject of the next cut. As arranged it is designed to give rapid alternating shocks.

Two powerful horseshoe magnets are mounted as shown. A pair of bobbins, such as those used on the legs of horseshoe electro-magnets, are carried by a vertical spindle so as to rotate between the opposing poles. The letters, N and S, seen on the magnet ends, denote the north and south poles respectively. The bobbins have, as cores, two bundles of iron wire, which should be annealed and oxidized. Each piece of wire should be long enough to nearly reach from face to face of the magnets.

As wire, Nos. 30 to 36 may be used. The bobbins may be two inches long, and wound with enough wire to fill them up to a diameter of one inch. Between every layer of winding a piece of paraffined paper must be smoothly wound. Shellacked paper

FIG. 42. MAGNETO-GENERATOR.

may be used instead, and each of the layers may then be varnished with alcoholic solution of shellac. The general precautions observed in winding the secondary of an induction coil must be followed here.

In laying on the windings the greatest care must be taken to avoid kinks, or sudden bends. From time to time the part wound should be tested with a galvanometer, as in the case of the induction coil, to see if it passes a current. If the wire breaks, the ends must be soldered after neat twisting together.

The wire on the bobbins must be wound in opposite directions, one right and the other left handed, exactly as in a horseshoe electro-magnet.

On the upper end of the spindle are an insulated collar and an insulated crown-wheel. The bobbins are connected together so as to give the current an opposite direction in each one. The connecting wire is made to lead diagonally from front of one to rear of the other. This leaves two free terminals. One is soldered to the collar, the other to the crown-wheel.

Two springs of copper, brass, or silver, press, one against the collar, the other against the teeth of the crown-wheel. Multiplying gear is applied to drive the mechanism, by turning the bobbins rapidly around in the magnetic field created by the magnets.

The springs are secured to insulated binding posts, to each of which flexible wire, or conducting cord, is connected. The other ends of the pieces have handles.

If, now, the hand-wheel is rapidly turned, while the handles are held one in each hand, or are applied to different parts of the body, a succession of rapidly succeeding shocks will be felt.

Should it be desired to have the impulses all run in the same direction, the commutator shown and described on page 58, must be used, instead of the collar and crown-wheel.

A well made magneto-generator, such as described, will give powerful shocks. If wound with coarser wire, No. 25, or thereabouts, and if provided with the commutator just alluded to, it will give quite current enough to heat fine platinum wire and decompose water.

Electric Artillery.

Explosions of gunpowder, or of hydrogen, or of coal gas, mixed with oxygen or air, can be produced by the electric spark, or by an incandescent wire. The cut shows what may be termed an electric mortar. It may be made of metal or of wood. Two wires, insulated from the material of the mortar, if the latter is of metal, are arranged as shown, approaching close to each other, but not touching within the cavity of the mortar.

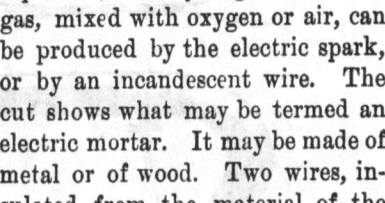

FIG. 43. ELECTRIC MORTAR

Such a mortar may be charged with powder, and if a spark from a Leyden jar, induction or spark coil, is passed through it, the powder will explode. A ball placed on the mouth, which is countersunk to receive it, will be shot into the air. A magneto-generator may be used to produce the spark.

The ignition by a spark is not always certain. It is a common practice to include in the circuit, if a Leyden jar is employed, a piece of wet cord, which makes the spark more efficient. The spark may be taken also directly from an electric machine.

It is better to produce these explosions by a wire heated by a current. For such, the simplest method

108   ELECTRIC TOY MAKING.

is to fit the barrel with a plug, which screws tightly into it, and through which the two wires, well insulated, pass as shown in the cut.

The wires protrude a little on the inner side, and

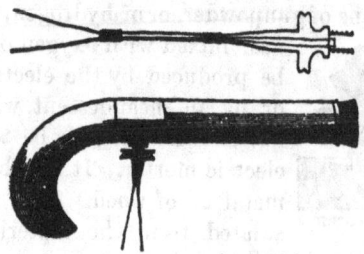

FIG. 44. ELECTRIC OR VOLTAIC PISTOL.

across from end to end of them a very fine wire, of platinum or of iron, is carried. It must be in good electrical connection with both, which is best insured by soldering. The copper wires may be No. 20 or thereabouts. What is the simplest, and really the best construction, is to make a plug of some non-conducting material, such as hard wood, and to thrust the bare wires through holes which, if in wood, may be bored with a brad-awl. The connecting wire should be very fine and the shorter it is the hotter it will get. If too great a current is employed the wire will be melted. It is well to test, by experiment, how many cups of the experimenter's battery are required to heat it to redness.

ELECTRIC ARTILLERY. 109

All this is a subject of calculation, and those who wish can readily work out the problem for themselves.

Such an apparatus may be called an electric primer. A pinch of gunpowder can be ignited by passing a current through the wire, immersed in or covered by it.

The voltaic pistol simply consists of a tube of brass with a handle and a side connection into which the plug screws. By holding it mouth downwards for a second or two, some inches above and over an open unlighted gas-burner, it will be charged with a mixture of air and gas. A cork is now thrust into its mouth; it is held pointed in the right direction, and a current is passed through the cap. The mixture explodes and drives the cork out. To produce a strong explosion, the proper mixture is about six of air to one of gas. Such a mixture may be made in a test tube or even in a bottle. One sixth of its volume of water is introduced and the tube or bottle is inverted, without loosing any water, into a basin of water with its mouth under the surface; the rest of the bottle is now filled by bubbling gas into it.

The pistol barrel is filled with water; it is inverted in the basin, and the contents of the bottle are introduced, bubbling through the water. It is removed, mouth downwards, and quickly corked, and all is ready for the explosion.

For an extremely violent report, a mixture of one

volume of oxygen to two volumes of hydrogen gas may be used.

It is obvious that many variations can be introduced in this experiment. A bottle may take the place of the pistol. The wires may be thrust through the cork, which will take the place of both the cap and cork. The bottle is best filled over water to secure the right mixture. On turning on the current the cork will be driven up to the ceiling.

In the same way India rubber balloons may be exploded. They must be partially inflated with oxygen evolved under pressure, and then about twice the volume of hydrogen is introduced directly from the

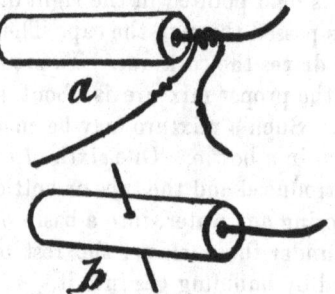

Fig. 45. Fire Cracker Explosions.

generating flask. A very small cork is arranged with the exploding wire connection. As the balloon is filled its neck is pinched with the finger well up from the end, and the cork is dexterously introduced.

Common fire crackers may be used as presented in

the cut to illustrate electric fuses. All that is necessary is to twist a fine wire around the projecting fuse of the cracker, as shown in the cut at a, or to transfix the cracker with a piece of fine wire, as shown at b. When a strong enough current is sent through the wire the explosion of the fire cracker will follow.

In "rain-making" experiments, conducted in the arid zone in the western United States, in the season of 1891, large balloons of combustible gas and oxygen were exploded by electricity in the hope of producing rain.

Electric Gymnastics.

A very clever idea has taken shape in the production of gymnastic apparatus, which in its use produces and administers electric shocks. The type of apparatus is of the weight-lifting kind, in which spade handles attached to ropes are pulled by the gymnast. The strings run over pulleys and weights are attached to their ends. By varying the weights the exercise may be made more or less severe, and by different movements a great variety of exercise may be derived from the comparatively simple apparatus.

The idea of applying electricity is to cause these movements to be productive of shocks. This can be effected in several ways. The first way to be described is by a magneto-generator.

The cords of the apparatus have wires running through them. The handles are metallic and are in electric or metallic communication with the wire. The magneto-generator has already been described. In the ordinary gymnastic apparatus the pulleys are fastened about six feet from the floor. At this point the generator is to be secured. From the pulley spindle a horizontal axle runs along parallel with the wall. The generator is placed in such a position that this axle comes in the prolongation of its own axle and three or four inches out from the wall. The axle passes through two strong journal brackets or pillars. Two pulleys with deep, wide grooves have fastened to them the handle cords. A third pulley has the weight-cord fastened to and wound around it a number of times.

Under this arrangement it is clear that, when the weight is up, the handles will be free to be pulled out to the full extent. If the weight descends it will unroll its own cord, and roll up the other two.

In these movements, the bobbin of the generator will turn with greater or less velocity, according to the way in which the apparatus is handled. If the wire handle-cords are connected to the terminals from the bobbin, the one who manipulates the apparatus will receive a series of electric shocks. This will be more violent as he works the apparatus more energetically.

The connection is easily managed. Perhaps the simplest way is by springs, which bear against insulated metal-coated drums or collectors.

ELECTRIC GYMNASTICS.

For this method two collars of wood, or other insulating material, are fastened to the axle, one for each handle-cord. The collars have a ring of brass around their peripheries. Each wire from a handle-cord is soldered, or driven firmly under the brass on one of the collars.

Copper or brass springs are attached to the base-board carrying the apparatus, which lies flat against the wall. There is one spring for each collar, and each presses against the metal coating of the collar. These springs are in electric communication with the terminals of the magneto-generator.

Thus arranged the generator terminals are in constant connection with the handles, and the person operating receives the desired electrical excitement. It is also possible to dispense with the commutator of the generator and simply connect the terminals from the rotating bobbins directly to the handle-wires. This gives, however, rather a slow succession of shocks.

Another way of arranging the system is to use an induction coil. Then the working of the apparatus is caused to make and break the primary circuit.

For this end, the general features of a rotating axle, with handle cord and weight-cord pulleys, is preserved. The same collars and springs are employed also. Upon the back-board an induction coil is mounted. Its secondary terminals are carried to

114   *ELECTRIC TOY MAKING.*

the two springs, thus being in electric connection with the handles.

The axle which rotates back and forth carries an insulated circuit breaking wheel of the general type of the one shown in the cut. As it has to work in

FIG. 46. CIRCUIT BREAKER.

both directions of rotation, the wire that strikes the teeth must be so bent and shaped as to work whichever way the wheel may rotate. Two springs press, one against the teeth, the other against the face or frame of the wheel, and connect with battery and primary.

A better arrangement is to mount a regular smooth surfaced commutator on the axle. This may consist of a wooden cylinder, to which are secured a number

ELECTRIC GYMNASTICS.

of slips of thin brass lying parallel with the axis. These should be so thin as to lie flush with the wood, or they may be inlaid, or embedded in it. Two small screws will fasten each piece. A ring of brass goes around one end of the commutator drum, being in good electrical connection with all the slips.

One spring is attached to the base so as to bear against the ring. Another spring bears against the drum to one side of the ring. From one spring a wire goes to one of the primary terminals of the coil. From the other spring a wire runs to the battery, and the other battery wire runs to the other primary terminal of the coil.

It will be understood, of course, that the coil is unprovided with an automatic circuit breaker, and that the manipulation of the apparatus by the gymnast, makes and breaks the primary circuit. This induces a current in the secondary, which, by the spring connections, wires and metallic handles, finds its way to the hands.

The coil should be provided with a movable core, or brass shielding tube, or else some arrangement for raising and lowering the battery plates should be provided in order to vary the strength of the induced currents.

The magneto-generator gives shocks varying in intensity as well as in frequency. The induction coil gives shocks of uniform intensity, varying in frequency. The objection to the latter is that it needs a battery.

It is also to be noted that the magneto-generator may be made to supply the proper current to the primary of an induction coil, and that the collecting collars may connect with the secondary of the coil. In this method, the characteristic alternating current of the generator works the induction coil to advantage, without any mechanical make and break device.

The primary of the coil thus used should have a large number of turns, from one-eighth to one-fourth as many as are in the secondary wire. The bobbins of the generator should be wound of the same sized wire as the primary of the coil. No. 24 wire would be a good size for both.

This disposition will increase the tension of the circuit, and will give more powerful effects, as the apparatus is more rapidly moved.

Ano–Kato.

The words ANO, KATO, are taken from the Greek, and mean *up*, *down*, and allude to the motions of the objects seen in the box. The cut shows its general features of construction. It is a shallow box whose bottom and interior sides are coated with tin-foil. A number of objects are made out of the lightest pith.

The latter may be of the pith of cornstalks, of elder pith, or, what is still better, of the pith of the dry stalks of the sunflower. Little men with jointed legs and arms, insects, jointed snakes, etc., are made out of the pith, and may be colored with a little red

ANO-KATO.

and black ink. The box is covered with a piece of glass.

If the glass is rubbed with a proper rubber, it becomes electrically excited, and attracts the objects in the box. As they rise, they touch the glass; and as

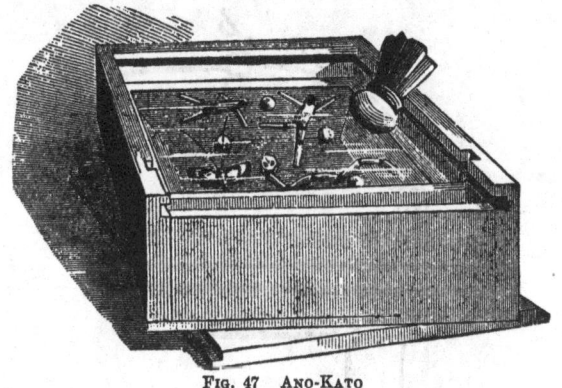

Fig. 47   Ano-Kato

they lie against it, becoming charged with the same electricity, are quickly repelled. They fall into the box and are discharged by coming against the tinfoil, which, for high potential difference, may be considered to be in electrical communication with the earth.

This operation goes on as long as the rubbing is kept up.

For the rubber, a pad of hair, or other material, around which a piece of kid glove is tied, is employed.

118 ELECTRIC TOY MAKING.

This may be made much more efficient by the use of some amalgam such as that used on electric machines.

Simple Experiments in Static Electricity.

Some simple experiments in static electricity are next illustrated. The first cut shows a modification

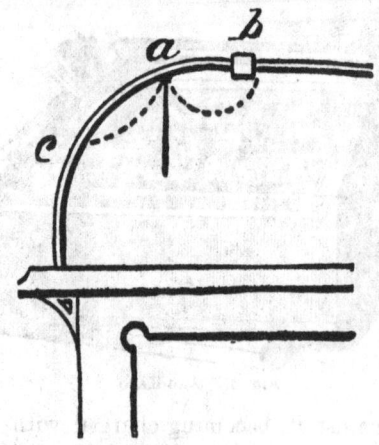

Fig. 48. GLASS SHOW-CASE EXPERIMENT.

of Ano-Kato. It is supposed to be especially adapted for use on the interior of a glass case.

A short silk thread, *a*, is stuck with a little bit of sealing-wax to the interior of a glass case, so as to hang down as shown in the full line. If, now, the exterior of the glass is excited by rubbing with a silk handkerchief, or other electrically efficient rubber, such as the pad just mentioned, the thread will be

EXPERIMENTS IN STATIC ELECTRICITY. 119

agitated and drawn in one or the other direction as shown by the dotted lines, *b, c,* following sometimes the finger. It is needless to remark that the movements thus excited, may, in their way, be very curious and amusing.

The next cut gives a view of India rubber balloons,

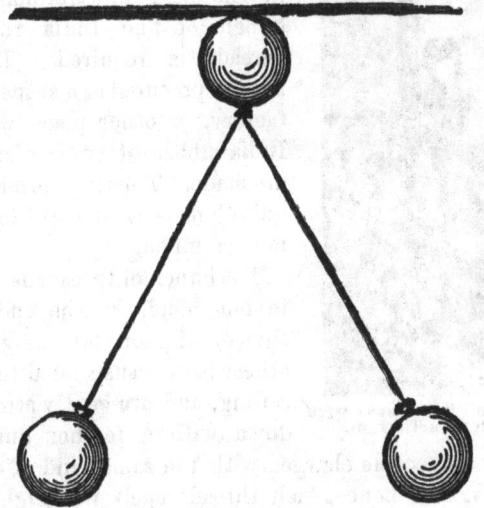

FIG. 49. EXPERIMENT WITH BALLOONS.

electrically excited. By striking these with a rubber of animal fibre, or tissue, such as a feather duster, they will become highly excited, and will tend to separate from each other. The balloons are the ordinary India rubber ones sold in the streets by peddlers.

It is said that three of them may be so excited that one will adhere to the ceiling, and carry the other two as shown. The latter are represented as repelling each other under the same excitement.

FIG 50   EXPERIMENT WITH RUBBER THREADS.

But of these simple experiments, one of the best is shown in the next illustration. A bunch of fine India rubber threads is required. These may be procured at a suspender factory, or other place, where India rubber interwoven fabrics are made. The threads may be quite long—six or eight feet is not too much.

The bunch of threads is held in one hand, by the end, as shown, if not too long, or otherwise are suspended to the ceiling, and are gently stroked down with a feather duster. They all become charged with the same kind of electricity, and hence, each thread repels its neighbor, and the whole bunch separates. The separation is quite persistent, and may last a long time.

CHAPTER VIII.

Hand Power Dynamo.

A HAND power dynamo is necessarily a rather feeble machine. But the construction of one is comparatively easy, and will give good practice, the benefits of which will be felt if a larger one is ever attempted.

For the sake of simplicity the well known "H" armature is adopted in the machine to be described, and the whole construction is designed to embody a very few parts.

In the illustration, the diagonally shaded parts show the section of the field magnet, wound with two coils of wire, as shown by the vertical lines near its base. The general construction or design is best seen in the cut. The following may be taken as general dimensions: Extreme length of field magnet, $4\frac{1}{2}$ inches; height, including feet, $4\frac{1}{2}$ inches; width, 2 inches. The elevation may be taken as on a scale of one-fourth the natural size.

As shown in the cut, an arm is cast on the magnet to hold the driving wheel. It is obvious that the arm can be dispensed with and a special standard used for this purpose.

122 *ELECTRIC TOY MAKING.*

Holes are drilled in the foot-flanges of the field-magnet, and it is screwed down to a base board about twelve inches long and six inches wide.

The field proper, or area within the pole pieces, the space in which the armature rotates, must be as exact a circle as practicable. The iron should be of

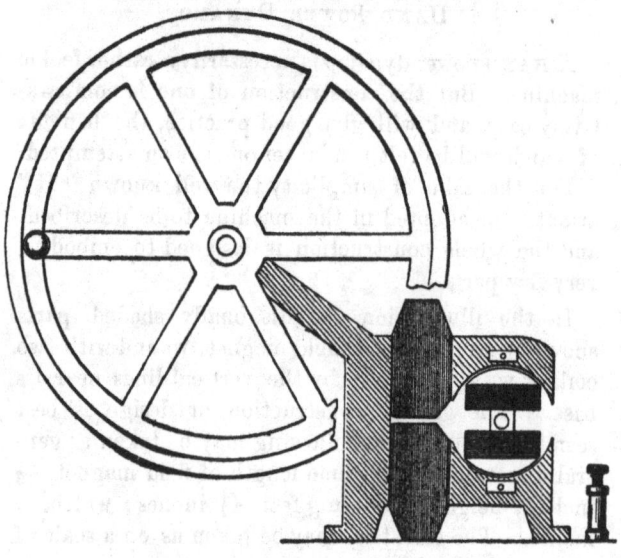

FIG 51. HAND POWER DYNAMO.

good quality and as soft as possible. Good cast iron will answer all requirements.

The interior surface of the pole pieces is sometimes

HAND POWER DYNAMO.

coated with tape, glued on. The portion to be wound with wire is smoothly coated in the same way. All is then ready for the winding.

One and one-half pounds of No. 21 silk-covered wire is used to wind the two field-magnet coils. The wire is weighed accurately and may be divided into two equal portions, each temporarily on its own reel. Otherwise it may be wound directly on one of the cores from a single reel, and the remainder weighed from time to time to ascertain when one-half has been employed. Then the other half is wound on the other core.

In either case the top core is first wound over the top and away from the operator, and as closely and evenly as possible. When partly wound, at short intervals, the winding is tested with a galvanometer and battery. One terminal of the battery is connected through a galvanometer with the coil terminal. The other battery terminal is touched to the iron of the field-magnet. If any deflection is produced the winding is defective in insulation, and is in electric contact with the field-magnet. It must be unwound and the trouble found and rectified.

In winding the superimposed layers, two pieces of tape, about one inch longer than the space wound, are to be laid on. After two or three thicknesses or layers of wire have been wound over it, the ends are turned in and over to be secured by the next winding. This is repeated so as to give a good winding surface and especially to prevent the under layers spreading. After a coil is wound it should be gently flattened down by blows with a wooden stick or mallet.

The second or lower coil is wound in the opposite direction over the top and towards the operator. If the wire with which the winding is done is in two pieces, two of the ends, the last of the upper and first of the lower coil must be connected by twisting and soldering, leaving two ends free. The latter go through holes in the base-board to two binding screws, one of which only is shown in the cut.

The armature is of "H" section and its spindle is journaled in two strips, which are screwed or bolted to the sides of the field-magnets. The places of attachment of one of these strips are indicated in the cut of the dynamo by two white rectangles with a bolt hole in the centre of each. These strips must be of brass or some non-magnetic material, and on no account of iron or steel.

The end view of the armature, giving also its cross section, is shown in the next cut. It may be of soft cast iron. It is far preferable, if possible, to build it up of washers of thin sheet iron annealed and oxidized, or with thin shellacked paper placed between each. In such case each piece must be perforated, but with a square or rectangular aperture, and strung upon a spindle which it closely fits. In such case special pieces must be used at the ends to secure the necessary projections or horns shown more clearly in the next cut, which represents the end view of the armature.

The edges of the armature are filed or smoothed off if necessary, and it is wound with one half-pound

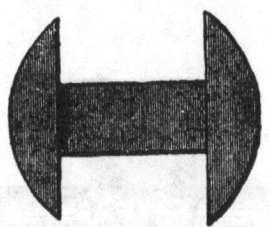

Fig. 52. End View of Armature.

of the same wire. The surface to be wound must be covered with tape, glued on. The winding is led or made to begin from the commutator end of the armature, and is interrupted where the spindle comes as shown in the cut of the dynamo, Fig. 51.

The commutator shown on the left of the spindle is a block of hard wood about three-quarters of an inch in diameter, and three-eighths of an inch deep. A tube of brass is driven over it and is screwed fast with short screws, which must not reach the spindle. The commutator is driven on to the shaft. The brass tube, after being screwed in place, is cut with two oblique and narrow cuts completely separating it into two halves. One of these cuts is shown on the commutator in Fig. 53.

The two terminals of the armature winding are soldered each to one of the commutator divisions.

A driven pulley one inch in diameter is fastened on the proper end of the armature spindle.

All these parts must be rigidly secured together.

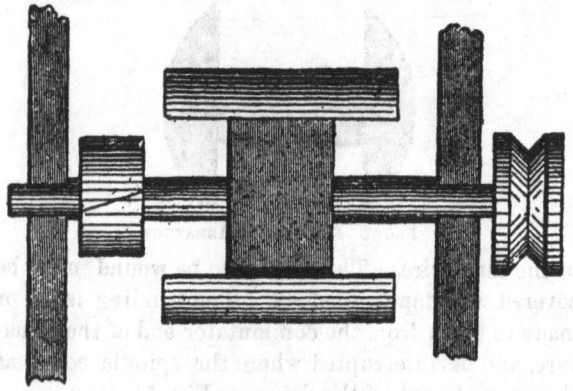

FIG. 53.—ELEVATION AND JOURNALLING OF ARMATURE, COMMUTATOR AND DRIVING PULLEY.

The armature spindle is two and one-quarter inches long, $\frac{5}{16}$ inch diameter, and the ends are turned down to $\frac{3}{16}$ inch for the bearings. It must turn freely in the space between the pole pieces with a clearance of about $\frac{1}{16}$ inch. This will exact very accurate centering. It is well to turn a fine groove in the centre of the cylindrical sectors of the armature and to wrap a few turns of wire around the windings,

HAND POWER DYNAMO.

and within the groove to stop the windings from displacement by centrifugal force.

Two springs or "brushes" of spring-tempered copper, about one-half an inch wide, are attached to the base board and bear against the opposite sides of the commutator. From each spring a wire may be carried to a binding-post. This gives a shunt wound machine. Or only one of the field-magnet terminals may be carried to a binding-post, the other connecting with one of the commutator brushes. The other commutator brush connects with the other binding post. This is a series wound machine.

The driving pulley is about ten inches in diameter, and like the driven pulley is grooved to receive a sewing machine belt.

The proper position of the commutator is found by trial, twisting it back and forth until the best results are obtained.

Such a dynamo, if properly constructed, will, at 1,600 revolutions, or at two and one-half turns of the driving-wheel per second, give about ten volts potential difference, and over an ampere of current. Two or three cells of bichromate battery will operate it as a motor, the driving belt being removed.

CHAPTER IX.

AN EASILY CONSTRUCTED MOTOR—SIMPLE ELECTRIC MOTOR—A SMALL ELECTRO MOTOR—ANOTHER SIMPLE MOTOR—SIMPLE ELECTRIC LOCOMOTIVE MOTOR — TELEGRAPH KEY — SOUNDER — MICROPHONE—TELEPHONE RECEIVER.

An Easily Constructed Motor.

This motor requires very little lathe work and, in fact, can be built without the use of a lathe.

The field magnet is of soft iron, ½ inch in diameter, and bent into horseshoe shape after heating.

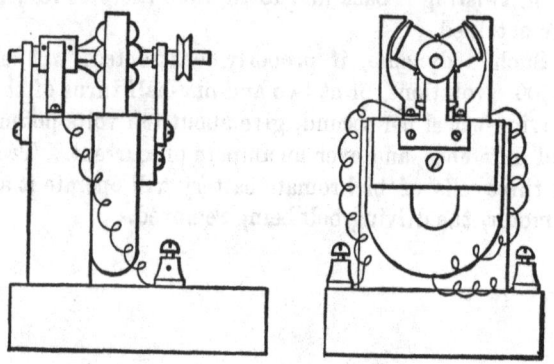

FIG. 54. AN EASILY CONSTRUCTED MOTOR.

AN EASILY CONSTRUCTED MOTOR.

The pole pieces are bored or filed out to just clear a 1½-inch armature.

The armature is of the three-pole type and should be made of laminations of thin soft sheet iron cut to the shape and size shown in Fig. 55. A simple and easy way to make these is shown here. A pattern is first marked off by using a pair of dividers to mark the outside circumference of the poles. Divide this circle into three equal parts, and draw a line from the center of circle to each of the three points on the circumference. These will be the center lines of the three poles of the armature.

Lay out, with the dividers, the three pole-pieces equally, using the three radial lines as center lines.

FIG. 55. ARMATURE LAMINATION.

When this pattern has been cut out and carefully filed to shape, it is used to mark out the other laminations. First, center-punch and drill a ¼-inch hole for the shaft, exactly in the center of the sample lamination.

Lay the pattern on the sheet of iron, and mark the position of the shaft hole. Drill this hole first.

Place the shaft through the holes in the pattern and sheet, and mark out the shape of the lamination with a sharp scriber.

The sheet iron pieces can be trimmed down to their outer shape with a pair of heavy shears, and the irregular portions cut out with a solid end punch, as shown in Fig. 56.

This punch can be made from a piece of tool steel about ¼ inch in diameter and 3 inches long. The point is filed down to about 3-16 inch in diameter, hardened, and tempered to a dark straw color.

FIG. 56. PUNCH.

Lay the sheet of iron on the end grain of a block of oak or other hard wood, and placing the point of the punch close to the line marked out for the shape of the finished lamination, give a quick, sharp blow with a hammer on the head of the punch. This will cut a round piece of sheet iron the size of the point of the punch without bending the iron out of shape.

Continue this operation along the lines marked out, letting the holes cut into each other slightly, and the irregular pieces required can be very readily and quickly cut out, leaving very little to be finished with the file.

Select a fresh spot on the block of wood for each hole cut out, otherwise the soft iron will be forced into a depression of the wood and be bent out of shape.

Sufficient laminations are required to build up a thickness of ½ inch.

AN EASILY CONSTRUCTED MOTOR. 131

When these are all cut out, assemble them on the shaft, with the pattern on the outside, and file the rough edges down to the size of the pattern.

The sharp corners should be filed off where the wire is to be wound on, and a layer of paper or other thin insulating material wrapped around. If paper is used, the iron should be shellacked first to make the paper stick to it.

The shaft is made of a piece of steel rod. Two small brass collars can be forced on the shaft.

Fig. 57 shows the construction of the commutator.

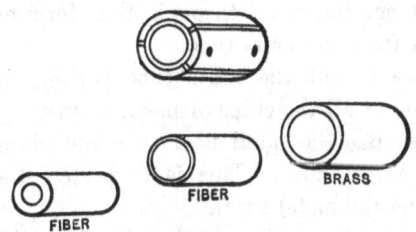

FIG. 57. DETAILS OF COMMUTATOR.

This is made from two pieces of fiber tubing and an outer tube of brass from which the segments are formed.

First, shellac the outside of the larger fiber tube and the inside of the brass tube and force them together.

At equidistant points around the circumference of

the tubes, at each end, drill holes for small brass rivets.

Escutcheon pins may be used for rivets, but the tops of the round heads must be filed down flat and the points put through the tubes *from the inside*. The points must be clipped off and riveted as each one is put in position.

To rivet them place a rod of iron or steel through the fiber tube and rest the rod on the jaws of a vise.

After the fiber and brass tubes are riveted, divide the brass tube into three equal parts around the circumference midway between the rivets, and with a hack saw cut the metal through, thus forming three segments from the brass tube.

Be sure to cut the brass tube entirely through and clean out all the chips of metal between.

Next shellac the small fiber tube and place it inside the larger tube. This is to protect the rivet heads from the metal shaft.

The commutator can now be placed on the shaft and the face turned off in a lathe. If the builder has no lathe, then file down the rivets and use the commutator without turning.

The fiber and brass tubing can be procured in such even and true shape that the turning is not an absolute necessity.

The bearings are cut out of 1-16-inch sheet brass. The size and shape are shown in the cuts.

AN EASILY CONSTRUCTED MOTOR.

The base and magnet support block are of wood, fiber or rubber, as desired.

The two pieces can be fastened together by screws passing through the base into the support.

The brushes are made from this brush copper and attached in the proper position on the support block by screws.

The field magnet is wound with four layers of No. 20 magnet wire. Begin and end the winding at the center of the curve of the magnet. Finish with a coat of shellac.

Wind the armature with No. 24 double-covered wire. Fill up the grooves with the wire, being careful to get the same number of turns on each of the three poles. Begin the winding on the side opposite the commutator and end on the commutator side.

When the three coils are wound, bring the three inside ends together and, after cleaning off the insulation, twist and solder them all together.

The outer ends of the coils are carried to the commutator and soldered to the segments, as shown.

Give the finished coils a good coat of shellac.

This is a very good design to "line up" after the parts are all completed, as will be seen from the cuts.

The circuit of the motor is from one binding post to the field magnet, thence to one brush and through the armature to the other brush and back to the second binding post. This is a "series" motor.

A grooved pulley can be used to drive other machines, or a fan can be mounted on the end of the shaft.

Simple Electric Motor.

This motor is not as strong as one having an armature wound with coils of wire, but is very easily constructed and can be used as a motive power for small toys, etc.

The base and support for magnet can be made of wood, fiber, or rubber, as desired. The field magnet is of ¼-inch soft iron and about 4½ inches in length, bent into the shape shown. To clamp the magnet down onto the support use a brass strap drilled for a small wood screw.

The armature is made from a piece of soft iron ⅛ by ¼ inch and about 1½ inches long.

A 3-32-inch hole for the shaft is drilled in the center of the armature.

The shaft should be about 2 inches long and carefully pointed at each end.

The armature can be forced onto the shaft and balanced to run steadily.

If one end of the armature bar is found to be heavier than the other when the shaft is supported on its pivots, that end should be filed until the armature will remain in any position in which it may be placed.

The bearings for the armature shaft are made of sheet brass of the shape shown.

SIMPLE ELECTRIC MOTOR. 135

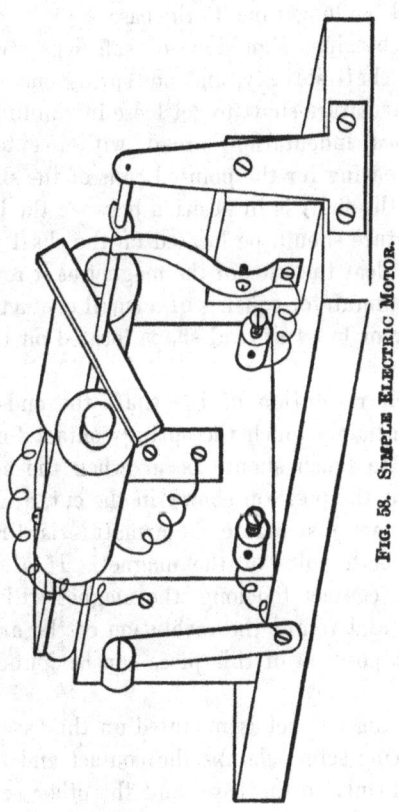

Fig. 58. Simple Electric Motor.

The shorter bearing is screwed to the magnet support, and the longer one to the base.

These bearings should be of sufficient stiffness to hold the shaft steadily, and not spring enough to allow the armature shaft to get loose in running.

A conical indentation is made with a center punch in each bearing for the pointed ends of the shaft.

When the shaft is in position between the bearings, the armature should be located on the shaft where it will just clear the ends of the magnet as it revolves.

The commutator consists of a small contact breaker of copper or brass of oval shape located on the shaft as shown.

At each revolution of the shaft the ends of the piece alternately touch the spring contact for an instant. The touch should occur when the armature is in about the position shown in the cut, and should break contact just before the armature is directly in front of both poles of the magnet. If allowed to remain in contact too long, the magnet will exert a back pull and retard the revolution of the armature. The exact position of this piece can be found by experiment.

The spring contact is mounted on the base by two screws. One screw clamps the contact and connecting wire firmly to the base, and the other screw adjusts the spring in its proper relation to the contact breaker.

The power of the motor can be doubled by making the armature in the shape of a cross instead of a straight bar, and arranging the contact breaker and spring with four points instead of two. This will make and break contact four times during each revolution of the armature instead of twice, as in the above description. A switch can be placed on the magnet support to stop and start the motor as shown.

The winding of the magnet coils consists of 400 turns of No. 26 single-covered wire in each coil. This may be wound directly onto the magnet by hand or wound over a fiber or paper spool and slipped onto the magnet afterward.

In either case the coils should be thoroughly shellacked and allowed to dry before handling.

The circuit is from binding post to one coil of the magnet, thence to the second coil, from magnet to bearing, and through shaft and contact to switch. From the switch to the second binding post.

When connected to a good-sized bichromate cell, the motor should run about two thousand revolutions per minute.

Small Electro-motor.

A very efficient little motor for driving model boats or locomotives, and for producing rotation of vacuum tubes, etc., may be constructed in the following manner: Procure a piece of soft hoop iron about ⅛-inch thick, ¾-inch wide, and 1 foot long; cut this into two equal pieces 6 inches in length; drill a 1-16-inch hole through the centre of each one; then bend each piece of the iron into the shape of the letter U, having the limbs 1¾ inches apart, and therefore about 2½ inches in length from the middle of bend to the end of limb. In one of these pieces, which is to be the fixed magnet, two other holes, in a line with the first, but near the edges of the iron, should be drilled, in order to enable the operator to fasten it to the base board when finished. A piece of sound mahogany or well-seasoned pine about 3 inches wide, ⅜-inch thick, and 10 inches long, should now be procured; and a piece about 3 inches square cut off one end and glued and screwed to the remaining 7 inches at right angles to it similar to a letter L. This piece, which forms the base board, may be stained or polished at the option of the maker. The next step is to wind the two U-shaped electro-magnets previously produced; great care, of course, being taken to cover the iron first with paper or tape to insulate the wire from the iron. Each magnet will require to be wound with 6 layers of No. 24 silk-covered wire; that is to say, between 6 and 9 ounces of the wire; the exact amount got on depending on the skill and neatness of the operator. The connection between the windings must be in the direction shown, viz., like a letter ∽. It will be well, in order to avoid joints, to measure off one-half of the wire intended to be laid on one electro-magnet, and without cutting it off from the remaining half, to wind one limb with the first half, the other limb being wound with the other half. In both electro-magnets, the winding should be begun near the bend; just at those portions where the limbs of the U begin to straighten. If, as directed, 6 layers of wire are got on, the finishing, or free extremities of the wires, will be found near the bend of the U's. At this point they should be carefully tied with thread to prevent uncoiling. If the operator prefers appearance to efficiency, nothing further need be done to the coils; but if, on the contrary, efficiency be the first consideration, it will be well to shellac the coils and let them dry in a warm place. Of course, in either case, the electro-magnets should be tested for insulation, before anything else be done. The next step is to fasten one of these electro-magnets (the one with the three holes drilled at the bend) to the upright piece of the base board, with the limbs parallel to the base itself, and at such a height that the other electro-magnet shall be able to rotate freely in front of it without touching the base; that is to say, the height from the base to the central hole of the fixed electro-magnet must not be less than 1¼ inches. The fixed electro-magnet must be fastened to the upright of the base board by means of two screws, one in each of the lateral holes previously drilled in the electro-magnet. Through the central hole of this same electro-magnet is passed a piece of stout brass wire about ⅛-inch diameter and ¾-inch long, and which has been filed down for about ¾ of its length to such a size that it can enter the hole in the centre of the electro-magnet, leaving a head about 3-16-inch protruding from this hole. In the centre of the head of this piece of brass is drilled a conical depression. This depression is to form one of the bearings in which the shaft or spindle which carries the movable electro-magnet will rotate. We will designate this the *back bearing*. The next operation consists in making a little pillar about 2 inches in height, from a piece of brass wire about ¼-inch in diameter. About ½-inch of one extremity of this pillar should be reduced by turning or filing to ⅛-inch in diameter, and a thread put on it by means of a die. At the upper extremity a hole must be drilled and tapped at right angles to the length of the pillar, and at such a height that when the pillar is screwed into the base board the hole shall be exactly in a line with the conical depression in the back bearing. This hole should be about ⅛-inch in diameter, and be fitted with a brass screw, to serve as the *front* bearing. The face of this screw must also have a conical depression drilled, corresponding to, and facing the one in the back bearing. The pillar may now be screwed into the centre of the base board at a distance of about 6¼ inches from the back bearing, with the screw which forms the front bearing in a line with and perpendicular to, the back bearing. If necessary, a small nut may be put at the lower extremity of the pillar screw which passes into the base board, so as to insure rigidity. In this case a hole must be countersunk at the under surface of the board, so as to allow the nut to lie flush with the board. A piece of steel rod 1-16-inch in diameter is now procured, and cut so as to be a little longer than the distance between the back and front bearings. This is to form the shaft or spindle of the motor. Its two extremities are filed to fine conical points, so as to run freely in the conical depression of the front and back bearings. These points can then be hardened by making redhot and plunging in cold water. The free electromagnet is now to be fitted to this spindle. For this purpose the spindle is pushed through the central hole at the back of the bend; should the existing hole not be large enough, it must be reamed out until the spindle will just enter. The spindle with the electromagnet on it is then placed between the bearings, the screw of the front bearing being tightened up to hold the spindle immovable. The movable electro-magnet is then placed with its poles facing, but not touching those of the fixed electro-magnet, a piece of stout cardboard, 1-16-inch thick, being placed between the poles to prevent actual contact. The magnet being held firmly in this position by the left hand, a file-mark is made with a sharp triangular file, at the point at which the bend of the electro-magnet touches the spindle. The spindle with the electro-magnet is now removed from between the centres, and the electro-magnet soldered to the spindle at the point just marked with the file. In order to solder effectually, the back of the bend of the electro-magnet, as also the inside of the bend, must be filed perfectly clean, and run over with the tinned soldering-iron, so as to get a coating of solder, before attempting to solder the spindle thereto. When this has been done, the movable electro-magnet should be again placed between its centres to see whether it runs freely before the poles of the fixed magnet, without either touching it on the one hand, or being more than 1-16-inch away from it on the other. If it should not do so, the soldering must be repeated until this result has been attained. A commutator is now made, and fitted to the spindle. It should be ½-inch long, and ½-inch in diameter, the central hole being a tight fit on the spindle. A small piece of hard fiber about ½-inch long is turned into a perfect cylinder about ⅜-inch diameter. A hole 1-16-inch diameter is put centrally through this, so that it can be made to fit tightly on the spindle. A piece of brass tubing, about 1-16-inch thick, ½-inch long, and ⅜-inch in internal diameter, is now driven on to the fiber cylinder. Two short brass screws, not reaching to the steel spindle, must now be procured, and, holes having been drilled at two opposite points in the diameter of the ring, and countersunk, the screws are inserted and tightly screwed down so as to hold the ring in its place. The brass tube or ring is now cut into two halves by giving two fine saw cuts across the ring at two points equi-distant from the screws just inserted. This completes the *commutator,* which is now ready to be slipped on the spindle. As the brass segments of this commutator must be carefully insulated from each other, from the spindle, and from he iron of the electro-magnet, very short screws must be used; and a small paraffined paper washer put over the spindle, against the electro-magnet, before the commutator is put on the spindle, and pushed up into its place, which is close against the outside of the bend of the movable electro-magnet.

A drop of shellac applied to the spindle where the commutator is finally to remain, will prevent it from slipping round. The commutator *must be so placed on the spindle, that when the limbs of the movable electro-magnet are exactly opposite the limbs of the fixed electro-magnet, the slits* of the commutator are *in a line* with the limbs; that is, they should find themselves at the two sides of the commutator, and *not* above and below. A small pulley, either of brass or wood, may be keyed or soldered to the spindle, to serve as a driving wheel. The free ends of the movable electro-magnet wires should now be cut a convenient length and soldered, one to each segment of the commutator. Two L-shaped springs (to serve as brushes) are now to be made out of a piece of very thin and springy brass, about 1½ inches in length beyond the bend, and ¼-inch wide. These are to be screwed down to the base board in such a position that they press squarely, yet not too heavily

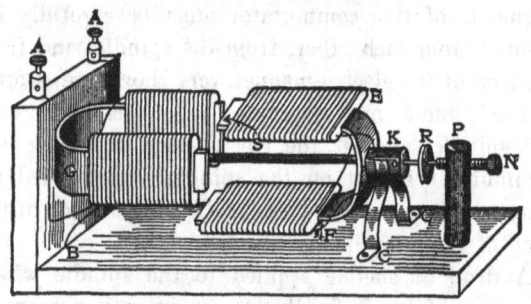

FIG. 59. SMALL ELECTRO-MOTOR.

on the opposite side of the commutator. Finally, one of the ends of the wires coming from the fixed electro-magnet G (see Fig. 59) is connected to a binding screw, A. The other end, is carried in a groove under the base board to the screw of the brush C, to which it is soldered, or otherwise electrically connected. The other brush, C, is connected by another wire passing under the board (and shown at B) to the terminal, A. The spindle carrying the movable electro-magnet and its attachment may now be put in its bearings, the brushes carefully adjusted, and the back screw, N, screwed up until the spindle can rotate *freely*, but without much play in its two centres, which should be kept oiled. If well made, this little motor will run well with a single Leclanché or pint bichromate cell, and at a furious speed with four cells.

Another simple motor to construct, and one which will immediately give us an insight into the principles involved in the electro-motor, is a modification of Dr. Ritchie's rotating electro-magnet. This may be very cheaply made from two bar-magnets, about 3 inches by $\frac{1}{2}$-inch by $\frac{1}{8}$-inch. These must be erected, as shown at S and N (Fig. 60), with opposite poles facing, on a base board, about $2\frac{1}{2}$ inches square. The lower poles should be connected together (underneath the board) by a strip of soft hoop-iron. This is not absolutely essential, but it conduces to the flow of the magnetism through the two bars. A steel spindle, A, about 3 inches long, may be made from a knitting-needle, the lower extremity being ground into a sharp point. At about an inch from the sharpened point is attached a hardwood collar, B, which can be fastened to the spindle either by a small key or by means of a little glue. Before being attached to the spindle, this collar must be furnished with two

146   ELECTRIC TOY MAKING.

brass segments, of which one is shown. The best way to make these segments is to fit a short piece of brass tube tightly over the hardwood collar. Drill two holes at opposite points of the circumfer-

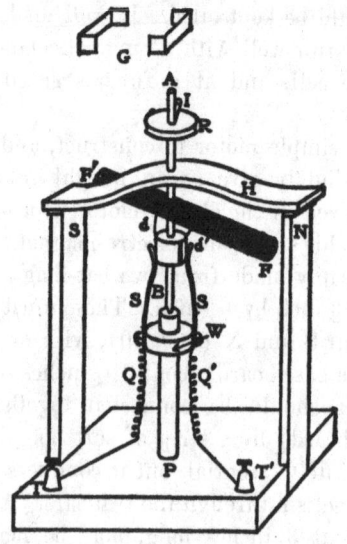

FIG. 60. VERTICAL SPINDLE-MOTOR.

ence, and countersink the holes. Two short flat-headed screws (not reaching to the central spindle) are then fitted to the holes and screwed home. By means of a fine fret-saw, the tube is now cut across at two equidistant points in the circumference (avoiding the screws), so that the collar is embraced by two brass half-circles, not touching each other at any point. This arrangement of collar and brass segments is known as a "commutator," since it serves to *commute* or change the direction of the current supplied to the machine. Just above this collar is tied a bundle, F, of fine soft iron wire, about ¼-inch in diameter, and of such a length as just to clear the magnet-poles, S and N. This bundle may be bound firmly together by wrapping round with thin ribbon from end to end, a little thin glue or shellac being used to hold the convolutions together. The upper part of the spindle, A, is then thrust through the centre of the bundle. The bundle must then be wound with two layers in one continuous length of No. 24 silk-covered copper wire, beginning at the middle, running to one end, returning by winding to the middle, then winding on to the other end, and finally winding back to the middle again; the two ends of the wire being brought out and soldered to the two segments of the commutator at $d\,d'$.

It is important that the slits in the commutator should be parallel with the length of the iron bundle, so that when the ends of the bundle face the poles of the bar-magnets the slits do so likewise. A short brass pillar about 1¼ inches long, made of ⅛-inch brass wire, is driven into the centre of the base board, as shown at P. By means of a ⅛-inch drill a conical hole is made at the top of this pillar, in which can turn, as in a centre, the pointed end of the spindle, A. At about ¼-inch from the top of this pillar is cemented, with glue, a wooden collar, W, to which are fastened, by means of short screws, *not* reaching to the pillar, two elastic brass springs, $S\ S'$, each facing one of the magnets, and reaching to press firmly and yet lightly on the split commutator. Two copper wires, $Q\ Q'$, connect these elastic springs (technically known as *brushes,* because they brush against the commutator) with the binding screws, $T\ T'$, by means of which the electro-motor can be coupled up to the battery or other source of current.

A piece of sheet brass, about ⅛-inch thick, and long enough, when slightly arched in the middle, to reach a little beyond each magnet pole, as shown at H, is now cut and adjusted to fit firmly on the top of the magnets. To do this, two little rectangular pieces of thin brass, 1-32-inch thick, of the shape shown at G, are soldered at each end of the crosspiece, H, on the under surface, so as to clip tightly the ends of the magnets. A central hole is now drilled through the cross-piece or "bearing," H, to admit the passage and free rotation of the spindle, A. A small grooved pulley, R, which may be either of brass or hardwood, about ½-inch in diameter, is then to be fastened to the spindle by means of a key as shown at I. By means of this pulley the power developed by this electro-motor can be transmitted wherever desired.

This electro-motor is described here (and recommended to be made), not because it is the most effective, but because it is very simple in construction, and because, if the reader makes one, so as to grasp the mode in which it acts, he will thoroughly understand the principles upon which all other electro-motors are constructed. We will, therefore, devote a few lines to the consideration of its action. Let us suppose that we begin by coupling up the *positive* pole of a battery (or other source of electricity) to the left-hand terminal T of the motor, the negative being connected to T', the coiled iron bundle standing with its extremities as shown in the figure, *not quite* facing the magnets. What takes place? The current passing along the wire Q, and entering the coil at *d,* converts the iron bundle into a magnet having a north pole at F', and a south pole at F. The consequence is that F' is attracted towards the magnet pole S, while F is similarly attracted by N. Under the influence of this double attraction, the iron bundle (which for the future we will designate the *movable* electro-magnet or *armature*) is pulled round towards the poles of the two magnets, carrying with it the spindle and pulley, A and R. When this armature arrives with its extremities exactly opposite the magnet poles S and N, since the springs or "brushes" $S\ S'$ are resting against the slits, *no current passes through the armature coil;* hence it ceases to be a magnet. And here it would stop, in this position, were it not for the fact that by the momentum gained by being pulled from its original position it passes a *little beyond* the central line, in so doing carrying the slits of the commutator a *little past* the springs or "brushes." Hence the spring S is actually resting against that section of the commutator which is attached to d', while $S\ S'$ is resting against d. The effect of this is that the current now enters the coil of the electro-magnet or armature F F', in the opposite direction to which it did before; therefore the nearer extremities of the armature are *repelled* by the poles of the magnets N and S, and pushed on in the same direction until they stand *across* the said magnets, when they enter the sphere of attraction of the opposite poles, by which they are consequently attracted as at first. Again, but with increased momentum, the armature flies past the attracting poles, breaking and renewing contact as before, and this series of rapid magnetization, demagnetization, and reversal of magnetism, with its accompanying rapid rotation, takes place as long as current is supplied.

Simple Electric Locomotive Motor.

This motor can be constructed with very little lathe work and few tools.

There are two magnets of the horseshoe type. These are mounted on the platform of the car, as shown in Fig. 61, and the armature revolves between them.

The magnets are made of soft iron 3-16 inch in diameter and 3 inches long, bent to the shape shown.

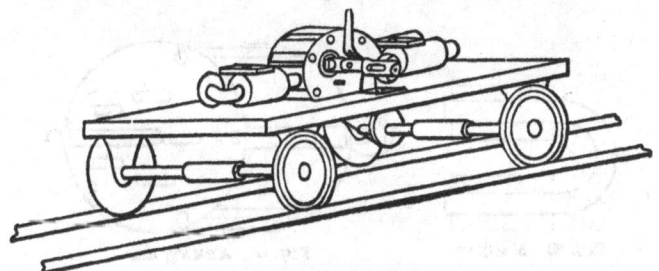

FIG. 61. ELECTRIC LOCOMOTIVE MOTOR.

The winding of the coils for these magnets should be ten layers of No. 28 single-covered wire. This should be wound on stout paper or fiber tubes and slipped onto the poles of the magnets after being shellacked and allowed to dry.

The armature consists of five strips of 3-16-inch square soft iron 1⅜ inches long mounted in two disks of brass 1½ inches in diameter and 1-16 inch thick, as shown in Fig. 63.

152   ELECTRIC TOY MAKING.

Divide the periphery of the disks into five equal parts, and drill five ⅛-inch holes just within the edge of the disks as shown.

Turn down the ends of the soft iron rods so that they will project slightly through the disks of brass and rivet the ends.

A hole for a ⅛-inch shaft must be drilled exactly in the center of the disks.

The commutator consists of brass pins projecting

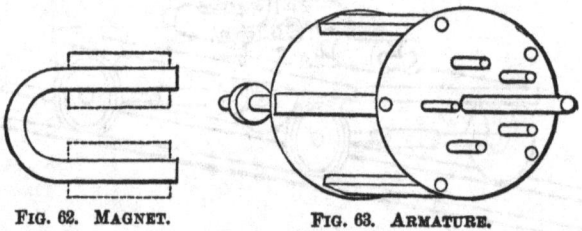

FIG. 62. MAGNET.   FIG. 63. ARMATURE.

from the side of one of the brass disks. The pins are the same in number as the soft iron strips of the armature, and should be located in a line with the center of the disks and the strips, and about ¼ inch from the shaft.

The brushes should be of very thin brush copper bent into a circle, and the ends riveted or screwed to the end pieces of the rocker arm, as shown in Fig. 64.

The rocker arm is made from a piece of sheet fiber

SIMPLE ELECTRIC LOCOMOTIVE MOTOR. 153

to insulate the brushes from the bearing. At each end is riveted, or screwed, an angle piece of brass to which the ring brushes are attached.

The hole in the center of the brush holder is drilled of a sufficient size to fit over the tube forming the bearing.

The reversing lever of the brush holders is an inverted T in shape, and is drilled with the same size of hole as the brush holder. In each end of the exten-

FIG. 64. BRUSH HOLDER DETAILS.

sions of the lever is drilled a hole which corresponds to holes drilled and tapped in the fiber piece of the rocker arm. When these parts are in position on the bearing and the screws inserted, they clamp the rocker arm and lever against the flat part of the bearing with sufficient force to hold the rocker arm in any position in which it is placed. The vertical lever should project above the armature far enough to be readily handled. The brush holder should be placed in such a position that the magnets will attract the strips of the armature just as they come near the poles, and cease attracting just as they are nearly in front of the poles.

To form stops for the rocker arm a small screw should be driven into the wood platform of the car under each end of the brush holder.

These can be adjusted to bring the brushes into the proper position—one for going ahead and the other for reversing. These will limit the movement of the rocker arm in both directions.

The bearings are of brass tubing soldered into the sheet metal supports, as shown.

These supports should be of brass 1-16 inch thick and bent at an angle at the base.

The platform of the car should be wood about 3 by 6 inches in size.

As the current is to be taken from the rails, it will be necessary to insulate the wheels of the two sides of the car. A simple way to do this is shown in Fig. 61.

The four wheels are each mounted on a short piece of steel rod for a shaft. The pieces are of such a length that when the wheels are in position on the rails, the ends of the axles will not touch each other. Two small fiber sleeves are drilled out, into which the inner ends of the axles are forced after they are placed through the sheet brass bearings of the car.

The construction of these parts is so clearly shown that further description is unnecessary.

The power is transmitted from the armature to the axle by a string belt running over two pulleys as shown.

The circuit of the motor is from one of the rails through the wheels and bearings to both of the magnets, thence to the bearings and commutator pins, from which it passes to the brushes, and from there by a flexible wire to one of the axle bearings on the opposite side of the car. From this point the current passes through one of the wheels to the second rail.

Telegraph Key.

A simple telegraph key, and one easily constructed by any amateur, is shown in the accompanying cut.

The base can be a piece of hard wood, fiber, or hard rubber, and the other parts can be elaborated to any degree to suit the taste of the constructor. The size of the base should be about 3x4 inches and ¼ or ⅜ inch thick.

The key proper consists of a strip of spring sheet brass about 2½ inches long and ½ inch wide.

One end of this strip is mounted on a block of the same material as the base, and the other end is provided with a knob for the fingers. This is secured by a round-head screw which passes up through the brass strip into the knob.

156   *ELECTRIC TOY MAKING.*

In the base directly under this screw is placed another round-head screw. When the key is depressed, these two screws meet and make a contact. Two binding posts are located on the back of the base.

The circuit is as shown by the dotted lines. The wires can pass along the surface of the base or pass down through and have grooves made on the underside to receive them.

If the screw heads become oxidized and do not

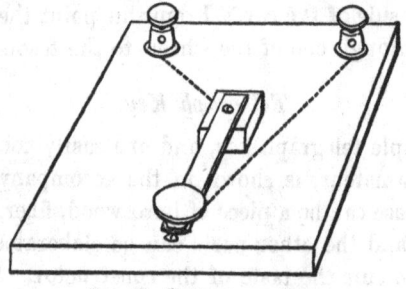

FIG. 65. TELEGRAPH KEY.

make good contact, they may be cleaned with fine sandpaper or emery cloth.

Sounder.

This instrument can be readily made by anyone having a few tools.

In the construction here shown, the cores of the electromagnet are formed of 5-16-inch flat-head wood screws about 2½ inches long. The heads of the magnet coils are made of ⅛-inch sheet fiber 1 inch in diameter. The two upper heads should have clearance holes in them, which will allow the screws to pass through freely, but the holes in the lower heads should be smaller to allow the thread of the screws to be forced into them, and thereby hold them at the proper position.

These heads, or washers, should stand square with

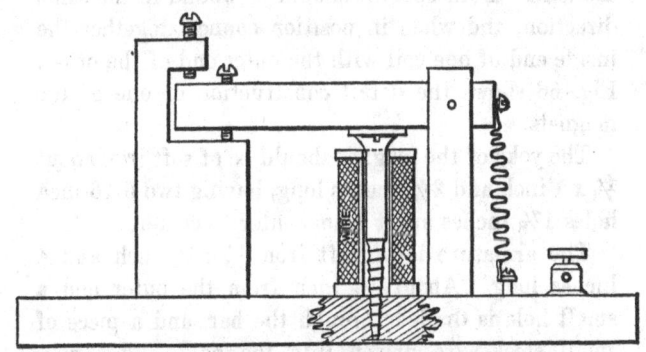

FIG. 66. SOUNDER, WITH DETAIL OF MAGNET.

the screws and at the same relative distance from the head. The body of the screws should be wound with a layer of paper shellacked, after which ten layers of No. 24 single cotton-covered magnet wire should be wound on each screw. The best way to do this winding is in a lathe; the point of the screw being held in the chuck and the wire spooled on between the washers. The more even the wire can be laid, the neater will be the appearance of the finished magnet. As soon as the wire begins to show an uneven surface, if a strip of stiff writing paper, cut just the width of the distance between the washers, is wound on over the under layer, it will form an even surface to begin the next layer on. It is always advisable to put a piece of this paper under the top layer of the wire. Both bobbins should be wound in the same direction, and when in position connect together the inside end of one coil with the outer end of the other. Fig. 66 shows the detail construction of one of the magnets.

The yoke of the magnet should be of soft iron about $\frac{1}{8}$ x 1 inch and $2\frac{7}{8}$ inches long, having two 5-16-inch holes $1\frac{7}{8}$ inches apart from center to center.

The armature is of soft iron $\frac{1}{8}$ x $\frac{1}{2}$ inch and 4 inches long. About $\frac{1}{2}$ inch from the outer end a small hole is drilled through the bar, and a piece of small steel wire driven into the hole. This wire should project about $\frac{1}{2}$ inch on each side of the bar. This forms the trunnion. The bearings for the trunnion are of hard wood or brass. If of wood they should be about $\frac{1}{2}$ inch square in section, but if of metal use the same size as the bar, $\frac{1}{4}$ x $\frac{1}{2}$ inch.

The height of the bearings should be about $2\frac{1}{4}$ inches above the base.

The parts can be attached at the bottom by turning down a tenon on the end to fit two holes drilled in the base, or a screw can be put up through into each bearing.

The bearings should be placed just far enough apart to allow a very thin washer between the bear-

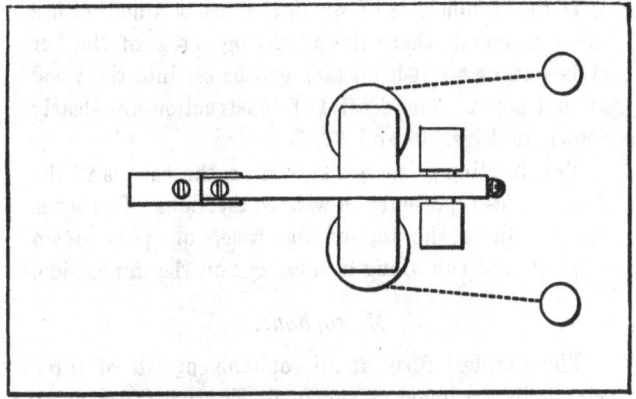

FIG. 67. TOP VIEW OF SOUNDER.

ing and bar on each side. On the end of the bar a hole is drilled and tapped for a small screw to hold one end of a coiled spring. The other end of the spring is attached to a screw directly underneath in the base, and by this latter screw the tension of the spring is adjusted.

At the inner end of the bar a machine screw is

placed at the position shown. This is for regulating the limit of travel of the bar in the downward direction.

The limit of upward travel is regulated by the screw placed in the standard. This standard is of brass or wood as desired, and can be attached at the bottom by two screws passing up through the base.

If the standard is of wood, it must be lined with a piece of metal where the adjusting screw of the bar strikes it, or a flat-head tack can be set into the wood at that point. The details of construction are clearly shown in Figs. 66 and 67.

Two binding posts are shown on the base, and the dotted lines represent the wire connections. The wires can lie along the top of the base, or pass down through and run along grooves cut on the under side.

Microphone.

The simplest form of microphone consists of three wire nails arranged as shown in Fig. 68.

The nails should be mounted on a thin box, such as the bottom of an inverted cigar box. This acts as a sounding board.

Two good-sized holes should be bored in each end of the box. The wires are twisted around the nails, as shown, and passed under the heads of the two screws in the end of the box. This is to prevent the wire from pulling the microphone out of position.

MICROPHONE.   161

The complete instrument is arranged as shown. A battery and telephone receiver are put in circuit between the binding screws.

The footsteps of a fly walking over the cigar box can be distinctly heard at the receiver, although the listener be several yards distant and in another room.

A more permanent arrangement is shown in Fig.

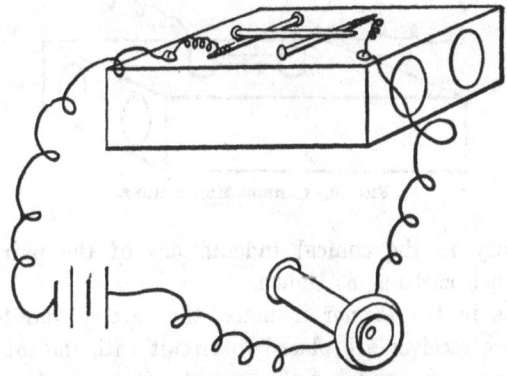

FIG. 68. WIRE NAIL MICROPHONE.

69. In this instance, instead of using three wire nails, three pieces of carbon are used.

Two of the pieces should be about ½ inch in diameter and about the same in height, with a hole drilled down through the center and a conical indentation on one side, as shown.

ELECTRIC TOY MAKING.

A screw is passed down through the center hole of each of the large carbons by which they are secured to a cigar box as a sounding board. The third piece of carbon should be about 3-16 inch in diameter and about 1½ inch or 2 inches in length, with both ends pointed as shown.

The pointed ends of this latter piece of carbon rest

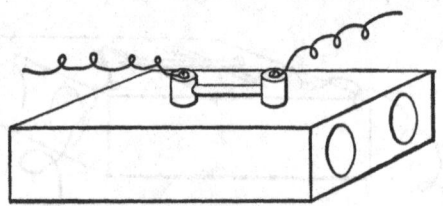

FIG. 69. CARBON MICROPHONE.

lightly in the conical indentations of the pair of ½-inch carbons, as shown.

As in the former instance, the battery and telephone receiver are placed in circuit with the microphone. The ends of the circuit wires are clamped under the screw heads passing down through the two carbon posts as shown.

Telephone Receiver.

This receiver is intended to be used with the microphones just described.

The materials necessary are a round bar magnet

TELEPHONE RECEIVER.

¼ by 3 inches, one drachm No. 36 silk-covered magnet wire, a piece of ferrotype plate 3 x 3 inches, two small brass terminals, a piece of round hard wood about 1 x 4½ inches, and a round wood box 2½ inches in diameter by 1¼ inches deep.

Drill a ¼-inch hole through the round piece of hard wood for its entire length to receive the magnet.

Drill a ¼-inch hole through the center of the bot-

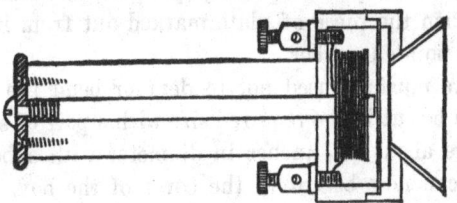

FIG. 70. TELEPHONE RECEIVER.

tom of the wooden box and, after squaring off the end of the round hard wood piece, glue the bottom of the box on the end of the piece, keeping the two ¼-inch holes in line.

On the opposite end of the hardwood piece is fitted a circular disk of brass about ¼ inch larger in diameter than the wood. Through the center is drilled a clearance hole for a No. 6 machine screw. Holes are also drilled and countersunk for three or four small brass wood screws by which it is secured in position.

The magnet should be drilled and tapped with No. 6 machine screw thread in one end.

The magnet should fit tight enough in the hole drilled through the wood piece that it will not turn readily when the screw is rotated for adjustment.

The piece of ferrotype plate can be fitted to the box as shown in cut. It must be held in the recess of the cover, and the two parts of the box must be fitted until they will just pinch the plate when shut together. A piece of stiff paper can be fitted first, and then the piece of plate marked out from it by a sharp pointed scriber.

Care must be used not to dent or bend the plate. It can be cut to the required size with a pair of shears. A hole about 1¾ inches in diameter with a beveled edge can now be cut in the cover of the box. This is for the ear piece, which should be of cardboard, pressboard or sheet fiber and glued into position.

A bobbin of pasteboard or fiber is made about 1 inch in diameter and ⅜ inch long.

This is placed on the end of the magnet bar in the relative position shown in the cut. After being shellacked the No. 36 wire is spooled on, leaving enough of the two ends projecting to be connected to the two binding posts as shown.

The parts are now ready to assemble.

First insert the magnet with its coil in position. Pass the No. 6 machine screw through the hole in the brass plate, and place the spiral spring over the screw, after which get these parts into position and start the screw into the thread in the end of magnet. The piece of coiled spring used should be quite stiff.

After the screw is fairly started, insert the wood screws and fasten the brass plate in position.

The ends of the No. 36 wire can then be soldered to the binding posts.

The magnet can be adjusted so that it will stand just below the diaphragm, and the latter can now be placed in position.

Place the disk in the recess of the box cover, and with a brush carefully shellac the two surfaces of the box where they fit together. Place the cover in position and press the parts together.

The final adjustment consists in loosening the screw in the end of the magnet until the magnet will touch the diaphragm.

This can be tested by gently tapping on the diaphragm with a pencil. As soon as the magnet touches the diaphragm, it will emit a dull, heavy sound.

Then turn the screw in the opposite direction very slightly, and test with the pencil. As soon as the diaphragm gives a clear sound, it is ready for use.

CHAPTER X.

MISCELLANEOUS RECEIPTS AND FORMULÆ.

Kookogey's Battery Solution.—Potassium bichromate, 227 parts; water, boiling, 1,134 parts; while boiling, add concentrated sulphuric acid, very carefully and slowly 1,588 parts; allow it to cool and to precipitate, decant for use. All parts are by weight.

Electropoion Fluid.—Mix one gallon sulphuric acid, concentrated, and three gallons of water. In a separate vessel dissolve six pounds of potassium bichromate in two gallons of boiling water. Mix the two solutions. Use only when perfectly cold.

Solution for Amalgamating Zinc.—Dissolve one part of mercury in a mixture of two parts nitric and four parts hydrochloric acid. After solution, add six parts more of hydrochloric acid. A few seconds immersion will amalgamate ordinary zincs, which may then be washed in clean water, and well rubbed. Amalgamation by rubbing with metallic mercury and dilute acid is generally simpler.

High Potential Battery.—Positive Element: Sodium amalgam in caustic soda solution.

Negative Element: A carbon plate in chloride of iodine.

The electromotive force of this battery is said to be about 4 volts. (See "Electric World," Vol. 6, No. 16).

Chloride of Iron Battery.—This battery corresponds in construction with the Bunsen battery, except that ferric chloride is used as the depolarizer in place of chromic acid. After it becomes polarized, by reduction of the ferric to ferrous chloride, it will recuperate on standing, as the air oxidizes the iron salt. As this action is slow, bromine was added to the depolarizing mixture. This gave a disagreeable odor. Another improvement was to add potassium chlorate with a little hydrochloric acid, which had very little odor and was found to work very well. The last combination is described by Thomas Moore, in the London *Chemical News*.

Potassium Permanganate Cell.—By using a solution of potassium permanganate and ammonium chloride in water as exciting fluid, with carbon and amalgamated zincs as the elements, a good open circuit battery is obtained. A warm and concentrated solution of potassium permanganate may be poured into exhausted and drained porous cells of Leclanchè batteries to regenerate them.

Dry Battery.—A good mixture for dry batteries is made up of : Plaster of Paris, 4 parts; zinc oxide, 1 part; saturated solution of zinc chloride, enough to make a thick paste. The Carl Gassner, Jr., patent specifies: Sal ammoniac, 1 part; plaster of Paris, 3 parts; zinc chloride, one part; water, two parts. All parts are by weight. A zinc can may be used as at once the cup and positive element; a rod of carbon is the negative element.

Smee's Battery.—This battery consists of amalgamated zinc positive and platinized silver negative plates, in a single vessel with a ten per cent. solution of sulphuric acid. To platinize the negative plate, dissolve a little platinum bichloride in water with a little hydrochloric acid, and decompose the solution by a battery, using a platinum plate as anode and the silver plate as cathode. This produces a deposit of platinum on the silver which facilitates the escape of hydrogen gas.

Platinized Carbon for Smee Batteries (WALKER).— The carbon plates are first purified by soaking them for some days in sulphuric acid diluted with three to four times its volume of water; a tinned copper conductor is then fastened to one by tinned copper rivets. The carbon is then platinized by electrolysis, the carbon plate being used as the cathode, the anode being either a platinum or carbon plate. The solution used is thus prepared: sulphuric acid, diluted with ten times its volume of water, is taken, and crystals of platinum chloride are added until the solution becomes of a beautiful straw yellow color. After the current has passed for about twenty minutes the plate is finished; it may be tested by using it as a cathode in the electrolysis of water; it ought to allow the hydrogen to escape freely, without sticking to it in the form of bubbles.

Porous Pots.—Minimum leakage with distilled water at 14°C., 15 per cent. in twenty-four hours.

Ebonite.—To keep ebonite in good order it should be occasionally washed with a solution of ammonia in water.

Non-Corrosive Soldering Fluid.—Mix water, 8 parts; glycerine, 1 part; lactic acid, 1 part. All by weight.

Low Temperature Solder.—For use when the parts to be soldered will not stand a high temperature. Finely divided copper (obtained by precipitating a solution of copper sulphate with zinc) is mixed with concentrated sulphuric acid in a porcelain mortar. 30 to 36 parts of copper are taken, according to the degree of hardness desired, and 70 parts of mercury are stirred in. When the amalgam has completely formed, it is washed with hot water till all traces of acid are removed. It is then allowed to cool.

When this composition is to be used, it is heated until it is of the consistency of wax, so that the surfaces to be joined may be readily smeared with it. When cold, they adhere very strongly.

To purify Mercury which has been used for amalgamating Zincs.—If one of the new low pressure distilling apparatus be not at hand, put the mercury in a deep vessel, put plenty of dilute sulphuric acid over it, and place a piece of carbon (a bit of an electric light carbon answers very well) into the mercury; weight it or tie it down so that there is good contact with the mercury; this arrangement sets up local action, and dissolves out all metallic impurities; do not carry the action too far, as you may dissolve some of the mercury in the form of mercury sulphates.

Gilt Plumbago (TABAURET).—For giving a conducting surface to electrotype moulds, .10 gr. of chloride of gold is dissolved in one litre of sulphuric ether, 500 to 600 gr. of plumbago (in fine powder) is thrown in, the whole is poured out into a large dish, and exposed to air and light. As the ether evaporates, the plumbago is stirred and turned over with a glass spatula. The drying is finished by a moderate heat, and the plumbago put by for use.

Soldering Wires (CULLEY).—To solder iron wires together, dissolve chloride of zinc (or kill spirit of salt with zinc), add a little hydrochloric acid (spirit of salt) to clean the wire. The rain soon washes off the excess of chloride of zinc. To solder iron and copper wires together the excess of chloride must be washed off, and the joint covered with paint or resin, or solder with resin.

For *unannealed* wires, solder at as low a temperature as possible.

The zinc solution, or spirit of salt, should never be used except for overhead out-door lines. All joints in covered wire, whether run underground or above ground, and all joints within doors, either in covered or uncovered wire, should be made with resin. No spirit of salt, either pure or killed with zinc, should ever be allowed in an instrument maker's shop or dynamo factory. Workmen will use it, if not watched. Its presence may often be detected by holding an open bottle of strong solution of ammonia (liquor ammoniæ) under a newly made joint; if it becomes surrounded with a slight white cloud or mist, spirit of salt in some form has been used.

Red Varnish.—For wood, interior of electro-magnet coils, galvanometers, etc., dissolve sealing-wax in alcohol at 90°; apply it with a pencil when cold in four or five coats, until the desired thickness is attained. It is better to use many coats than to make the varnish thick.

Covering of the External Wires of Large Electro-Magnets.—Large electro-magnets are generally wound with copper wire, covered with a double layer of cotton. The outside layer is hardened by painting it with cold, thick gum-lac varnish. It is gently roasted before a charcoal brazier. The layer thus formed is extremely hard. It is filed smooth, polished with flax and fine pumice powder, and finally varnished.

Cement for Induction Coils.—The proportions vary

very much but generally approximate to the following formula:

Resin,	2 parts.
Wax,	1 "

For hot countries slightly increase the proportion of resin.

Insulation of Wires for Telegraphy and Telephony (C. WIEDEMANN)–Prepare a bath of potassium plumbate by dissolving 10 gr. of litharge in a litre of water, to which 200 gr. of caustic potash have been added, and boil for about half an hour; it is allowed to settle and decanted. The bath is now ready for use. The wire to be insulated is attached to the *positive* pole of a battery or electroplating dynamo, and a small plate of platinum attached to the *negative* pole is dipped into the bath. The peroxide of lead is formed on the wire, and passes successively through all the colors of the spectrum. The insulation becomes perfect only when the wire assumes its last color, which is a brownish-black.

This perfect insulation may be utilized for galvanometers or other apparatus.

Chatterton's Compound.—For cementing together the layers of gutta-percha in cable cores, an excellent insulator of fairly low inductive capacity.

Stockholm Tar,	1 part.
Resin,	1 "
Gutta-percha,	3 "

Is also used for filling up the interstices of shore-end cables. Its density is about the same as that of gutta-percha, but its inductive capacity is less.

Joints of Gutta-percha Covered Wire (CULLEY).— Exact perfect cleanliness. Remove the gutta-percha for about four centimètres, clean the wire with emery paper, twist the wires together for about two centimètres, cut the ends off close, so as to leave no point sticking out. Solder with resin and good solder containing plenty of tin. The gutta-percha is then split, and turned back for about 5 centimètres, the soldered joint is covered with Chatterton's compound, and the gutta-percha on each side of it is warmed and manipulated until the two sides join. The joint is finished with a hot soldering iron, taking care to smooth it off well, without burning it; it is then covered with another layer of Chatterton's compound. A sheet of gutta-percha is then taken, warmed at a spirit lamp, and drawn out carefully so as slightly to diminish its thickness. Whilst both gutta-percha and Chatterton's compound are warm, the sheet is laid on the joint, and moulded around it with the thumb and forefinger. The joint is then trimmed with scissors; the edges kneaded in and smoothed down with a hot iron. When the joint is cold, another coating of Chatterton's compound is applied, and covered with a longer and broader piece of sheet gutta-percha. The whole is then covered with a final coating of Chatterton's compound, spread with the iron, and polished by hand when cold, taking care to keep the hand well moistened. It is indispensable to obtain intimate and perfect union between the new gutta-percha and that which covers the wire. A much neater and cleaner joint can be made by introducing the two wires into a little sleeve of tinned iron, fixing it to the wires by compressing it as a metal tag is fixed to a lace, and afterwards soldering; no points are then left sticking out at the ends of the joint.

Cement used by Gaston Planté for his Secondary Batteries is run *hot* on the corks and connecting strips of the secondary cells to prevent the acid from creeping.

Turner's Cement,	1,000 parts.
Tallow, or Beeswax,	100 "
Powdered Alabaster,	250 "
Lampblack (to color it black),	2.5 "

Waterproofing Wooden Battery Cells (SPRAGUE).—When the boxes are quite dry and warm, they are smeared over inside with a hot cement, composed of four parts of resin and one part of gutta-percha, with a little boiled oil.

It may be noted that the addition of boiled oil improves all substances used for this purpose which contain pitch, marine glue, or other viscous solid, tending to prevent them from flowing.

Watertight Decomposition Cells for Electrotyping (E. BERTHOUD).—A well made vat of oak may last for twelve or fifteen years, if it be smeared inside with the following composition:

Burgundy Pitch,	. .	1.500 parts.
Old Gutta-percha in small shreds,		250 "
Finely Powdered Pumice-stone,		750 "

Melt the gutta-percha, and mix it well with the pumice-stone. *Then* add the Burgundy pitch. When the mixture is hot, smear the inside of the vat with it. Lay it on in several coats. Roughness and cracks are smoothed off with a hot soldering iron. The heat of the iron makes the cement penetrate into the pores of the wood, and increases its adhesion. The vat will stand sulphate of copper baths, but not baths containing cyanide.

Cap Cement.—For joining glass tubes to brass caps and fittings, and for similar purposes, cap cement is thus made: Five parts, by weight, of resin are melted with one part of yellow wax; one part of finely powdered venetian red is stirred into the melted mass. To apply, both surfaces are warmed enough to melt the cement, but not too hot.

Electrical Cement.—For similar purposes to those to which "Cap Cement" is applied, the following (Singer's formula) cement may be used: Rosin, five parts; beeswax and red ochre, of each 1 part; plaster of Paris, $\frac{1}{4}$ part. A cheaper formula gives rosin, 14 parts; red ochre, 2 parts; plaster of Paris, 1 part.

Composition for Cushions of Ano-Kato, and of Frictional Electric Machines.—Canton advises the use of an amalgam of zinc and tin. Kienmayer gives the following formula: equal parts of zinc and tin; melt, and add twice the weight of alloy of mercury. When the rubbed plate or cylinder is of vulcanite, the amalgam must be softer than when it is of glass. In France they generally use *mosaic gold* (bisulphide of tin). The amalgam must be reduced to fine powder, and applied by the aid of a little hard grease.

Solution for Paper for Chemical Telegraphs.—One part saturated solution of ferrocyanide of potassium, one part saturated solution of nitrate of ammonium, two parts water.

To Make a Hole in Glass.—Make a circle of clay or cement rather larger than the intended hole; pour some kerosene into the cell thus made, ignite it, place the plate upon a moderately hard support, and with a stick rather smaller than the hole required, and a hammer, strike a rather smart blow. This will leave a rough-edged hole, which may be smoothed with a file.

To Cut Glass With Scissors.—Glass may be cut under water with great ease, to almost any shape, with a pair of shears or strong scissors. Two things are necessary for success. First, the glass must be kept quite level in the water while the scissors are applied; and secondly, to avoid risk, it is better to perform the cutting by taking off small pieces at the corners and along the edges, and to reduce the shape gradually to that required. The softer the glass, the better it cuts. The scissors need not be very sharp.

Direction for Making Lacquer.—Mix the ingredients and let the vessel containing them stand in the sun, or in a place slightly warmed, three or four days, shaking it frequently till the gum is dissolved, after which let it settle from twenty-four to forty-eight hours, when the clear liquid may be poured off for use. Pulverized glass is sometimes used in making lacquer, to carry down the impurities.

Lacquers for Brass.—1. Seed lac, dragon's blood, annatto, and gamboge, each 4 ounces; saffron, 1 ounce; alcohol, 10 parts.

2. Turmeric, 1 pound; annatto, 2 ounces; shellac and gum juniper, each 12 ounces; alcohol, 12 ounces.

3. Seed lac, 6 ounces; dragon's blood, 40 grains; amber and copal triturated in a mortar, 2 ounces; extract of red sanders, ½ drachm; Oriental saffron, 36 grains; coarsely powdered glass, 4 ounces; absolute alcohol, 40 ounces.

4. Seed lac, 3 ounces; amber and gamboge, each 2 ounces; extract of red sanders, ½ drachm; dragon's blood, 1 drachm; saffron, ½ drachm; alcohol, 2 pints, 4 ounces.

5. Turmeric, 6 drachms; saffron, 15 grains; hot

alcohol, 1 pint, draw the tincture and add: Gamboge, 6 drachms; gum sandarac and gum elemi, each 2 ounces; dragon's blood and seed lac, each 1 ounce.

To Clean Old Brass-Work for Lacquering.—Make a strong lye of wood ashes, which may be strengthened by soap lees; put in the brass-work, and the lacquer will soon come off; then have ready a mixture of aqua fortis and water, sufficiently strong to take off the dirt; wash it afterward in clean water, and lacquer it with such compositions as may be most suitable to the work.

To Polish Brass.—Rub the metal with rottenstone and sweet oil, then rub off with a piece of cotton flannel, and polish with soft leather. A solution of oxalic acid rubbed over tarnished brass soon removes the tarnish, rendering the metal bright. The acid must be washed off with water, and the brass rubbed with whiting and soft leather. A mixture of muriatic acid and alum dissolved in water imparts a golden color to brass articles that are steeped in it for a few seconds.

To Make Bronzing for Wood.—Grind separately to a fine powder, Prussian blue, chrome yellow, raw umber, lampblack, and clay, and mix in such proportions as will produce a desired dark-green hue; then mix with moderately strong glue size.

MISCELLANEOUS.

To Bronze Wood.—First coat the clean wood with a mixture of size and lampblack; then apply two coats of the green-colored sizing as in last receipt, and lastly with the bronze powder, such as powdered Dutch foil, mosaic gold, etc., laid on with a brush. Finish with a thin solution of castile soap; and, when dry, rub with a soft woolen cloth.

To Protect Steel From Rusting.—It has been found by experiment that an electro-deposited coating of nickel protects the surface of polished steel completely from rust. Swords, knives, and other articles of steel liable to exposure may be coated with nickel without materially altering the color of the metal.

To Clean Brass.—If there is any oily substance on the brass, boil it in a solution of potash or strong lye. Mix equal quantities of nitric and sulphuric acids in a stone or earthen vessel, let it stand a few hours, stirring it occasionally with a stick, then dip the brass in the solution, but take it out immediately and rinse it in soft water, and wipe it in sawdust till it is dry.

To Make a Leclanché Battery.—Place in a porous cell a rod or plate of carbon, and fill the cell with coarsely powdered black oxide of manganese and clean coke or retort carbon. Seal the top, leaving two holes for the air to escape when the cell is set up. This cement, for the top, may be made of black pitch. Place the porous cell in any old jar of the same height containing a saturated solution of sal-ammoniac and a rod of zinc.

To Polish Brass Ornaments Inlaid in Wood.— The brass-work must first be filed very even with a smooth file; then, having mixed some very finely powdered tripoli with linseed oil, polish the work with a rubber made from a piece of old hat or felt, as you would polish varnish, until the desired effect is produced. If the work be ebony or black rosewood, take some elder-coal, powdered very fine, and apply it dry after you have done with the tripoli. It will add to the beauty of the polish.

INDEX.

ALARM or safe protector. 69-72
Amalgamation of zincs in batteries 15
Amalgamating zinc, solution for 166
Ano-Kato 116-118
Ano-Kato in show case, 118, 119
Armature, Page's rotating. 56-59
Armature, Page's rotating, its commutator... 58
Armatures, rolling 28, 29
Artillery, electric 107-111

BALLOONS, experiment with rubber.. .....119, 120
Bars, steel, to magnetize. 23-28
Batteries 9-22
Batteries, bichromate .. 11, 12
Batteries, copper sulphate, 9, 10
Batteries, dip 11, 12
Batteries, miniature, from electric light carbons.. 13
Batteries, primary in general 9
Batteries, sal ammoniac.. 10
Batteries with electric light carbons........ 15-20
Battery from a tomato can 20, 21
Battery, gravity 10
Battery, high potential . 166
Battery, Lalande—Chaperon 21
Battery, Leclanché 10, 11
Battery, silver chloride.. 13-15
Battery solution, Kookogey's 166
Battery solution, Trouvé's 12
Battery troughs of wood. 22
Bell, the tolling......... 65-67
Bell, the vibrating...... 67-69
Bells, electric.......... 65-72
Boat, magnetic.......... 36
Burglar alarm 69-72

CAP cement 175

Carbons, applying paraffine to 16
Carbons, electric light in batteries 15-20
Cells, materials for.... 21, 22
Cement, electrical....... 175
Cement for induction coils 171
Cement used by Gaston Planté 174
Chatterton's compound... 172
Chloride of iron battery.. 167
Circle, the magic...... 42, 43
Circuit breaker, pendulum 83-85
Circuit breakers for induction coils.. ......97, 98
Coil, pendulum motor... 46-49
Coil to magnetize with... 27
Coils, induction and spark 89-104
Coils, induction, condensers of. 99-101
Coils, magnetizing, to make 40-42
Coils, spark and induction 89-104
Condensers of induction coils 99-101
Copal gum for coils...... 42
Copper oxide in battery. 20, 21
Core of coils, how made 89, 90
Covering of the external wires of large electromagnets 171

DANCER, the electric..... 73-76
Dancer, the electric, battery required for...... 76
Directions for making lacquer 177
Drum, the magic....... 76-79
Dry battery 167
Dynamo, hand power .. 121-127

EASILY constructed motor 128
Electrical cement 175
Electric artillery...... 107-111
Electric bell, key for..... 67

INDEX.

Electric bells 65-72
Electric dancer 73-76
Electric dancer, battery required for.......... 76
Electric gymnastics ..111-116
Electric hammer 79-82
Electric insects 82-87
Electric insects, circuit breaker for 83-85
Electric insects, mercury switch for.......... 86, 87
Electric light carbons in batteries 15-20
Electric locomotive...... 59-64
Electric locomotive motor 151
Electric mortar...... 107-111
Electric motors 46-64-134
Electric pistol....... 108-110
Electro-magnet from gas-pipe 38, 39
Electro-magnet, Joule's.38, 39
Electro-magnets 37-45
Electro-magnet, solenoid 39, 40
Electro-magnets, their construction 37-40
Electro-motor, small..... 137
Electropoion fluid........ 166

FIRE cracker explosions and fuses 110, 111
Fishes, magnetic 36
Force, lines of, followed by polarized needle...29, 30
Formulas and receipts, miscellaneous 166-180
Foucault's experiment.. 32-34
Fuses, fire cracker.... 110, 111

GENERATOR, the magneto 104-107
Gilt plumbago 170
Gluing coils........... 41, 42
Gymnastics, electric..111-116

HAMMER, the electric.... 79-82
Hemispheres, magnetic...43-45
High potential battery... 166
Hopkin's electric insects.82-87
Hopkin's magic drum....76-79

INCANDESCENT lamp.... 87, 88
Induction coil, Recordon's 102-104
Induction coils....... 91, 104
Induction coils, condensers of 99-101
Insects, electric......... 82-87

Insects, electric, circuit breaker 83-85
Insects, electric, mercury switch for 86, 87
Iron scraps in battery.... 20
Insulation of wires...... 172

JACK-STRAWS, magnetic.30, 31
Joints of gutta-percha covered wire............ 173
Joule's electro magnet..38, 39

KEEPERS of magnets...27, 28
Key for electric bell...... 67
Kookogey's battery solution 166

LALANDE-CHAPERON battery 21
Lamp, incandescent...87, 88
Lamp, platinum, self-regulating 87, 88
Leclanché battery, to make 179
Locomotive, the electric..59-64
Low temperature solder.. 169

MAGIC circle 42, 43
Magic drum 76-79
Magnetic fishes, swan, boat, etc. 36
Magnetic hemispheres....43-45
Magnetic jack-straws...30, 31
Magnetic pendulum 32-34
Magnetic swan 36
Magnetic top 31, 32
Magnetizing by a dynamo 25
Magnetizing by an electromagnet 25, 26
Magnetizing by a permanent magnet 24, 25
Magnetizing coils, to make 40-42
Magnetizing, Elia's method 27
Magnetizing, Jacobi's method 26, 27
Magnetizing steel bars..23, 28
Magnetizing with a coil.. 27
Magneto-generator 104-107
Magnets, compound 26
Magnets, ill effects of jarring and filing........ 28
Magnets, permanent 23-36
Magnets, to preserve ...27, 28
Mahomet's coffin 29, 30
Mahomet's coffin with solenoid 40

INDEX.

Mayer's floating needles.34, 35
Microphone 160
Miscellaneous receipts and
 formulæ 166-180
Miscellaneous toys...... 73-88
Mortar, electric 107, 108
Motor, easily constructed. 128
Motor, multipolar....... 51-56
Motor, multipolar, its commutator 53-55
Motor, pendulum coil....46-49
Motor, Recordon magnet.49-51
Motor, simple electric locomotive 151
Multipolar motor....... 51-56
Multipolar motor, its commutator 53-55

NEEDLES, Mayer's floating 34, 35
Non-corrosive soldering
 fluid 169

OXIDE of copper in battery 20, 21

PAGE's rotating armature.56-59
Page's rotating armature,
 its commutator........ 58
Page's solenoid magnets.. 39
Paraffine applying to carbons 16
Pendulum circuit breaker.83-85
Pendulum coil motor....46-49
Pendulum, the magnetic..32-34
Pistol, electric or voltaic 108-110
Platinized carbon for Smee
 batteries 168
Porous pots............. 169
Potassium permanganate
 cell 167

RECEIPTS and formulas,
 miscellaneous 166-180
Recordon's induction
 coil 102-104
Recordon magnet motor..49-51
Red varnish............. 171
Rolling armatures...... 28, 29
Rolling armatures, repulsion of.............. 29
Rotating armature,
 Page's 56-59

Rotating armature,
 Page's, its commutator. 58
Rubber balloon experiment 119-120
Rubber thread experiment 120

SAFE protector 69-72
Show case, Ano-Kato,
 118, 119
Simple electric locomotive
 motor 151
Simple electric motor.... 134
Small electro-motor...... 137
Smee's battery.......... 168
Soda, caustic, in battery.. 20
Soldering fluid, non-corrosive 169
Soldering wires......... 170
Solenoid electro-magnet.39, 40
Solenoid of electric hammer 81, 82
Solution for amalgamating zinc 166
Solution for paper for
 chemical telegraphs.... 176
Sounder 156
Spark coils 89, 91
Static electricity, simple
 experiments in 118-120
Steel bars, to magnetize.23-28
Swan, magnetic......... 36
Switch, mercury, for electric insects 86, 87

TELEGRAPH key 155
Telephone receiver....... 162
Tolling bell............ 65-67
Top, the magnetic...... 31-32
Toys, miscellaneous..... 73-88
Trouvé battery solution.. 12

VIBRATING bell 67-69
Voltaic pistol........ 108-110

WATERPROOFING wooden
 battery cells 174
Watertight decomposition
 cells for electrotyping.. 174
Wires, insulation of..... 172
Wooden battery cells,
 waterproofing 174

ZINC, amalgamation of, in
 batteries 15

www.ingramcontent.com/pod-product-compliance
Lightning Source LLC
Chambersburg PA
CBHW011341090426
42743CB00018B/3414